The Edge of Christmas
Carving Christmas Whimsies

Paul F. and Camille J. Bolinger

Schiffer Publishing Ltd
4880 Lower Valley Road, Atglen, PA 19310 USA

Dedication

At the time I promised our publisher, Mr. Peter Schiffer, that he could have this book, all kinds of other forces in my life gathered and tried to thwart the effort. While the effort was delayed, it was not stopped—thanks to the help of my wife, Camille, who dropped all other activities to do her part. Of course, I couldn't let her down. Thanks Camille.

Acknowledgments

We tried to find a way to let poor Pat McChesney off the hook for this book, but he refused. He actually thinks photographing this work is fun. So, for as long as he enjoys the work, we will continue to entertain him by doing it. Pat's ability to take pictures that actually make these carvings look good is delightful; the man is a wizard.

Library of Congress Catalog Card Number: 98-87455

Designed by Randy L. Hensley
Type set in DomBold BT/Bodoni Bk BT

ISBN: 0-7643-0687-1
Printed in China

Contents

Published by Schiffer Publishing Ltd.
4880 Lower Valley Road
Atglen, PA 19310
Phone: (610) 593-1777; Fax: (610) 593-2002
E-mail: Schifferbk@aol.com
Please visit our web site catalog at
www.schifferbooks.com or write for a free catalog.
This book may be purchased from the publisher.
Please include $3.95 for shipping.

In Europe, Schiffer books are distributed by
Bushwood Books
6 Marksbury Rd.
Kew Gardens
Surrey TW9 4JF England
Phone: 44 (0)181 392-8585; Fax: 44 (0)181 392-9876
E-mail: Bushwd@aol.com

Please try your bookstore first.

We are interested in hearing from authors
with book ideas on related subjects.

Introduction

One of the things you will notice when you come into our workshop is that we have an extremely wide range of carving and painting styles. If you have seen our Schiffer woodcarving books, then you know what I mean.

Our first successful carvings were one-of-a-kind original Father Christmas figures carved from basswood and hand-painted with artist oils. These pieces as well as Camille's oil painting methods are shown in our book "Carving and Painting an Heirloom Santa."

Later, we moved into carving figures that are more whimsical and humorous. In the books "Carving Humorous Santas" and "Halloween Carving", both also Schiffer published, you can see the wide range of funny, whimsical, and cute topics we chose to feature.

Taking a different approach, "Edge of Christmas" shows a collection of shelf sitting figures designed to catch the eye and add an extra touch of merriment to Christmas decorating.

Accompanying the patterns and photos in the book are design notes and hints to help readers see the pieces through my eyes, as I was designing and creating them. Design, after all, is the key to any project. The desire to carve is simply not enough; once inspired, you must develop the design and then create it. Here, I offer you many designs, but more importantly I also provide you with the tools to develop and refine your own designs. Copying my designs will reward you, but inventing imaginative and innovative designs of your own will be the real thrill.

Special Note

During the carving of this book, I wore my "I'm A Woodcarver" T-shirt. Pat and I intended to get a full front shot of the shirt, but somehow we never did get a real photo of it. This shirt and another woodcarver shirt were designed for me by my brother, Bruce, who is a professional cartoonist. I have included the designs for the two shirts here so you can see what I was wearing.

I received so many comments on the shirts over time that my brother and I eventually offered them to woodcarvers in "Chip Chats" magazine - now many woodcarvers around the country have one. If you are interested in a shirt for yourself or your carving buddies, send me a note at my home address: Paul Bolinger, 4405 S. Echo Ct., Spokane, Wa. 99223.

Chapter One
The Edge of Christmas

The first name I came up with for this book was "Christmas on the Edge" since that is the way we always end up celebrating Christmas. Because we are in the Christmas "business," the Christmas season ends up being one of intense pressure for us. We rarely have the time to get ready to celebrate; we are always living on the edge.

Our business consists of several different activities, including creating original woodcarvings, resin cast commercial reproductions, writing books, and even working on some other non-related efforts. In some years, during the Christmas season, the requirements on me for travel have meant that I was gone for most of the time - from mid-October until Christmas. When I was home during the season, I would carve as many originals as possible, so Camille could work on them while I was away. Between the two of us, we are always extremely busy trying to fill orders. Some years our output amazes me.

Our original carvings in the Schiffer book "Carving and Painting an Heirloom Santa" require from me and also from Camille quite a bit of time. We sell them at shows for private collectors, take mail orders, and also wholesale some each year. Despite that each one may take several days to produce, we have produced as many as 120 or so in a year and as few as 50 in other years. In fact, 120 in a year is actually an average of 1 carving every 3 days.

In the past 5 years, I have spent a significant amount of time designing smaller pieces for our resin cast collection known as "The Ho, Ho, Ho Gang." When we first undertook this collection, I imagined populating the collection with carvings that would remain there for several years. I was terribly wrong. One of the big requirements of the commercial Christmas business is to keep things "fresh." Each year a major part of every collection is retired and, consequently, must be replaced. Under these circumstances, we were never actually able to catch up. There were always ideas we had that just didn't make it because we would run out of time. And, of course, we were always in a rush to turn in the maximum number of carvings that we could, so the collection could look as complete as possible.

In getting the pieces ready for this book, I felt some of the same pressures. I guess living on the edge is just another way of life and I had better get used to it.

These pieces I call "shelf sitters" or "edge sitters" because each one is designed to sit on the edge of a shelf, ledge, or mantle. Though the individual pieces themselves are wildly different, this unifying element holds the collection together. Also, since our eyes are trained to expect things to reside on the shelf and not hang over the edge, setting the figures upon a shelf or ledge attracts the eyes of the observer.

In my house, lots of books and other things cram the shelves. But, no matter how much there is, the crisp clean line of the shelf is never interrupted. Take a look at your own shelves.

Interrupting the running line of the shelf is what helps to make these pieces so eye-catching. Other elements, such as the intensity of color on a piece and the use of other items such as wire and metal in the design of a piece also help but it is their placement on a shelf that really makes them stand out.

The coloring of our original heirloom Santas is very "Old World" with faded oil painted finishes to suggest Christmas past. That look works very well for the expensive one-of-a-kind carving that goes into making these family treasures. See them for yourself in the Schiffer book "Carving and Painting an Heirloom Santa."

In "Carving Humorous Santas," the color scheme used for the pieces is more intense and up-to-date, with somewhat of a country flavor added to the coloring, though not enough to cause the pieces to be classified as strictly country.

In this book, the colors used for the "Edge of Christmas" collection are especially bright with many highlights and contrasts. With my blessing, Camille did this in order to make the pieces stand out even more when displayed on crowded shelves. The idea is to catch the eye with the bright color and then hold the interest of the observer with the added details.

In the past, my own prejudices have restricted me from adding non-wood elements to carvings. Originally, I felt that the nature of carving was to be "pure" and to do everything from wood. Over the years, I have come to enjoy the way adding other elements to a design can make it much more interesting.

In these designs, you can see how the items added to the designs enhance them and give a feeling of "whimsy" to the pieces. The use of wire, metal, or softer elements such as ribbon in combination with the wood makes for an interesting piece. So, when thinking up your own designs, go ahead and consider putting on the extras for flair.

Chapter Two
Patterns and Design Considerations

In this chapter, I provide the patterns for the pieces and discuss the preparation and thought process that went into designing each of them.

One overall design consideration to keep in mind is the requirement that the pieces sit at the edge of a shelf or in some cases actually overhang the shelf. To meet this requirement and make sure each piece will balance on the edge of a shelf, I designed the pieces so that enough weight would remain on the shelf to keep the pieces from tumbling over. In any design that you modify or generate on your own, always make sure enough of the piece sits back from the edge to balance whatever hangs over.

Another important design consideration is that the pieces have a perfectly flat surface to rest on; this is needed for stability. For this, I cut out the designs in layers, gluing the layers together before carving. In this way, I could cut the pieces from dimensioned and surfaced stock, which would allow me more easily to incorporate a nice flat edge into the design.

Certainly, a single piece of thicker stock may be used for the carving of your designs. Remember a nice flat surface (I call it the baseline) is still needed for each piece and a right angle must be carved into the piece so that something can hang over the edge.

Deciding to cut out several pieces and glue them together was an idea I found much easier said than done. When drawing the patterns, I first had to draw the designs as they would look when finished and then "disassemble" the piece in my mind into layers of 1/2" or 3/4" thickness each, so that the layers would add up to the same piece when glued together. Believe me, I redrew these patterns several times before they came out right. Each layer in the pattern is numbered from the back of the carving to the front. If you cut the layers out and glue them from layer #1 forward, you should get a pretty complete workpiece to start carving on.

In most of these designs, because the pieces will be resin cast, I made the back flat and plain in order to keep the cost down. You can detail the back on your pieces if you wish. In fact, you could add an entire layer at the rear and put on extra details. However, since the pieces are intended to sit in a certain way on the shelf, the back generally will not be visible.

For those pieces, I cut the layers out with a handheld jigsaw, which caused them not to overlay exactly. It doesn't really make a difference though, since you will carve away the rough edges anyway. If you carefully draw and cut then you should get a reasonable fit among the layers. The glue lines disappear during carving and the glue presents no particular problems.

In the design notes, I have included a sketch of how the glued up piece will sit on a shelf. Look at the notes and study the drawing and you will see that I recommend a 2/3 to 1/3 distribution of weight so that at least 2/3 of the weight will hold the piece on the shelf, leaving 1/3 to dangle over. Also note the emphasis on grain orientation. Two key elements are highlighted - stability and grain orientation. Now let's look at some actual designs.

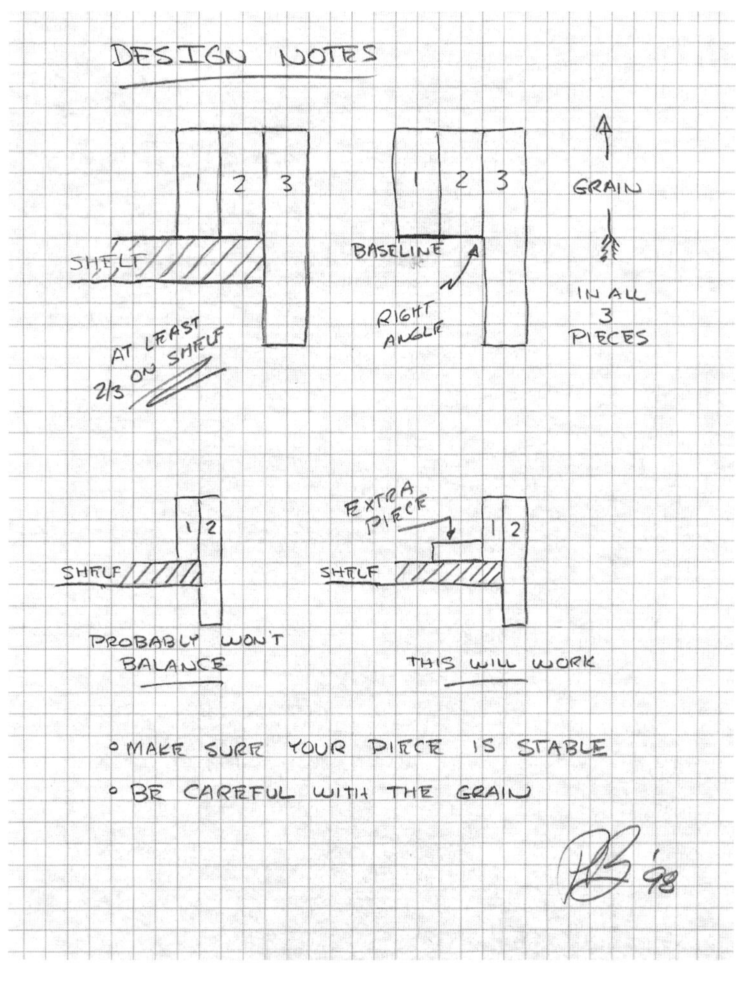

"Mr. Moose"

I'm not really sure if this fellow is a Moose or a Reindeer. If he were a reindeer his antlers would definitely be different. He started out in my mind to be a Reindeer and I don't know how he came out as a Moose. As you see from the pattern, the Moose is carved from 5 layers that have been glued together. Layer 1 is the farthest back from the front, giving you his arms and his antlers. Layer 2 provides the area for the face and fills in the body. Layer 3 provides some big knees for the Moose. Pieces 4 and 5 are identical and are the legs. Note that you will glue the legs to layer 3 so that they face forward. Also, note on the pattern where I indicated the "baseline." I always make sure this line exists along a straight edge. On this design I made sure that the grain ran up from the baseline, but the other direction would also work. Whichever way you choose, be consistent layer to layer or you will have problems. (Note: In the final Moose piece for the book, I eliminated the knee section and still came out with a good carving. Layer 3 in the carving would have to be a little deeper, but much the same.)

You can see that "Mr. Moose" rests on a large flat area made up of the baselines of 1 and 2, plus 3 if you use that piece in your design. This gives him an area of approximately 1 1/2" x 3" as a nice flat bottom.

I did not do much carving on the face. With these designs often "less is more" since you will paint the face on as you like it. I carved away his head to leave a nose and also made some cheeks and ears. Camille did the rest with paint.

Camille painted this Moose in a red outfit with polka dot mittens and polka dot pants. Red and green are great Christmas colors, while the moose himself looks good in light brown with the dark brown antlers. I really like the way Camille made him look like he had gotten caught up in a string of bells; the bells aren't too posed or stiff. He almost has a look to him like he might have just stumbled in from the annual Moose Christmas party.

This is the Moose with the string of bells snaggled in his antlers. He's got a great smile and I think the freckles are a cute addition. Note how his knees are angled in, which gives him a little bit more carefree posture.

This side view of the Moose shows the shape of his face, the depth of the carving, and the flatness of the back. Note that 2/3 of the Moose sits on the shelf while 1/3 hangs over.

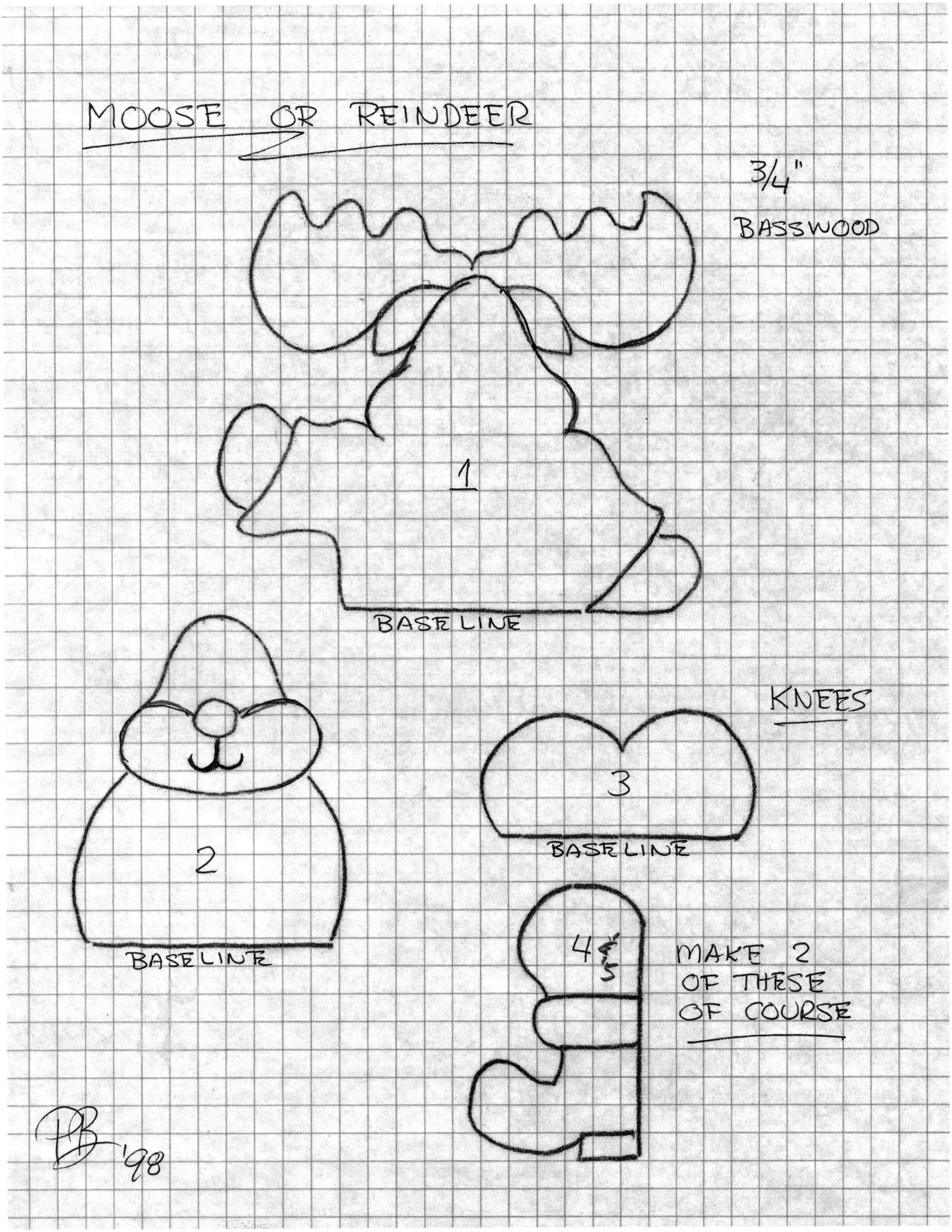
MOOSE OR REINDEER
3/4" BASSWOOD
1
BASELINE
2
BASELINE
KNEES
3
BASELINE
4 & 5
MAKE 2 OF THESE OF COURSE
PB '98

"Christmas Bear"

Looking at the pattern for "Christmas Bear," you see that he is made from 3 layers. Layer 1 is the body and left leg of the bear. Layer 2 is more body with the face also. Layer 3 contains the arm, other leg, and boot. You could easily turn the other leg the opposite direction and get a great look. I had to make a choice and went with the leg looking like I sometimes see my son, Jake, sitting with his leg dangling. Aren't kids and Teddy Bears a lot alike?

The baseline for the bear gives him flat spots on 2 of the 3 cut out layers, so 2/3 of the carving will sit on the shelf. Note: The pattern I am giving you has the bear facing toward you. I think this will make a more interesting carving.

I barely carved a face for the bear so Camille could play with it. Since my bear faces to the side, the face isn't as critical as it would be if facing forward. If your bear faces toward you, it will require some more detailed carving on the face to give it some shape. I like the green and polka dot vest and the fancy boots Camille gave this fellow. Also, I like the heart on the wire pole. My original design for this bear had him holding a fishing pole with a fish on the end of the line. That would make a neat piece too. You can modify this design as you wish. You might try a different hat style, turn its head slightly, or a different dress. I have provided some design variation drawings in the book to help you modify the design.

This top view of the Christmas Bear shows the depth of the carving and how he sits on the shelf.

This is the front view of the Christmas Bear even though he does face to the side. Note that the face is painted and not carved. His posture is cute and the heart Camille added is great. The pattern I put in the book faces forward but you can carve him the way I did if you wish.

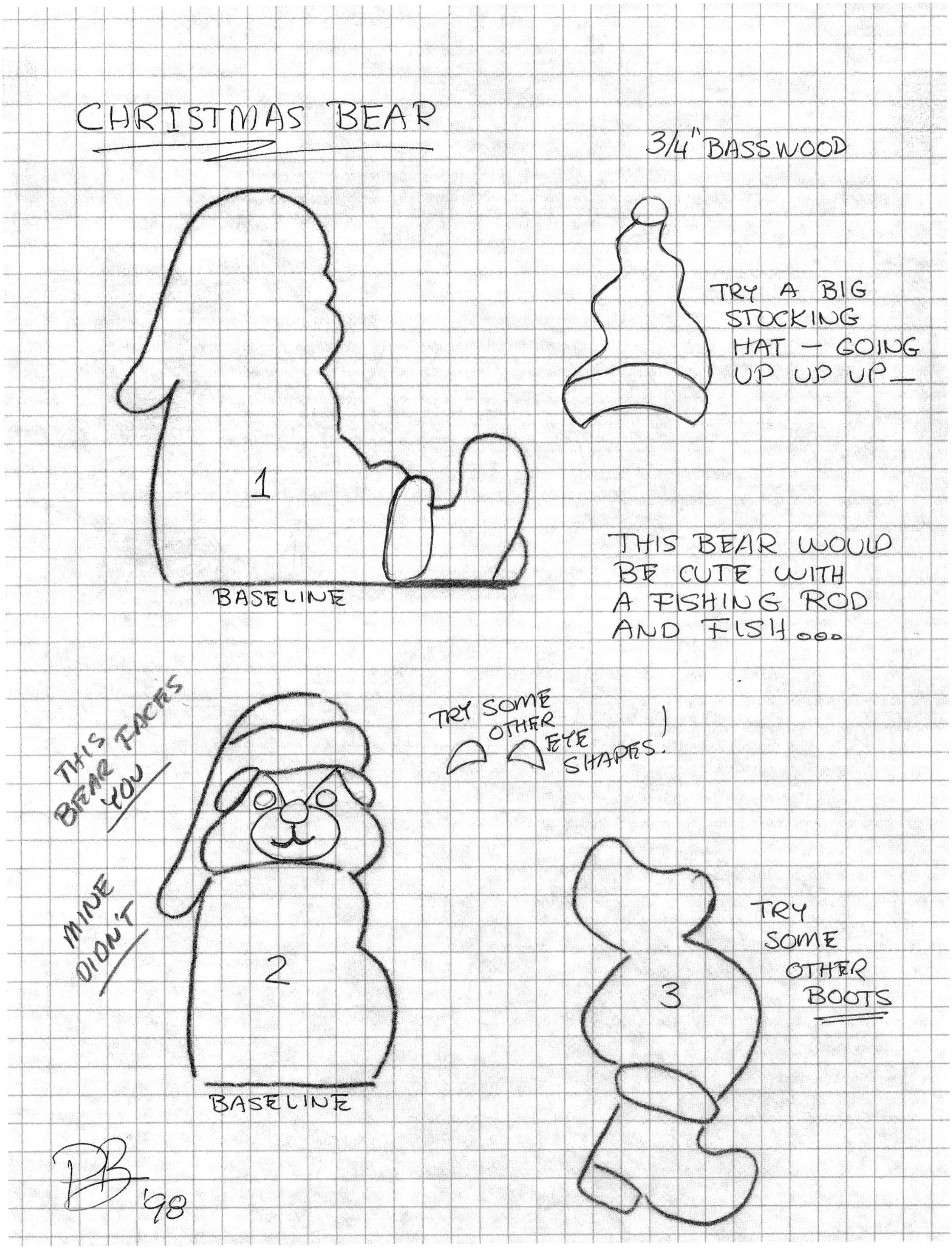
CHRISTMAS BEAR
3/4" BASSWOOD
TRY A BIG STOCKING HAT — GOING UP UP UP—
1
BASELINE
THIS BEAR WOULD BE CUTE WITH A FISHING ROD AND FISH...
THIS BEAR FACES YOU
MINE DIDN'T
TRY SOME OTHER EYE SHAPES!
2
BASELINE
3
TRY SOME OTHER BOOTS
DB '98

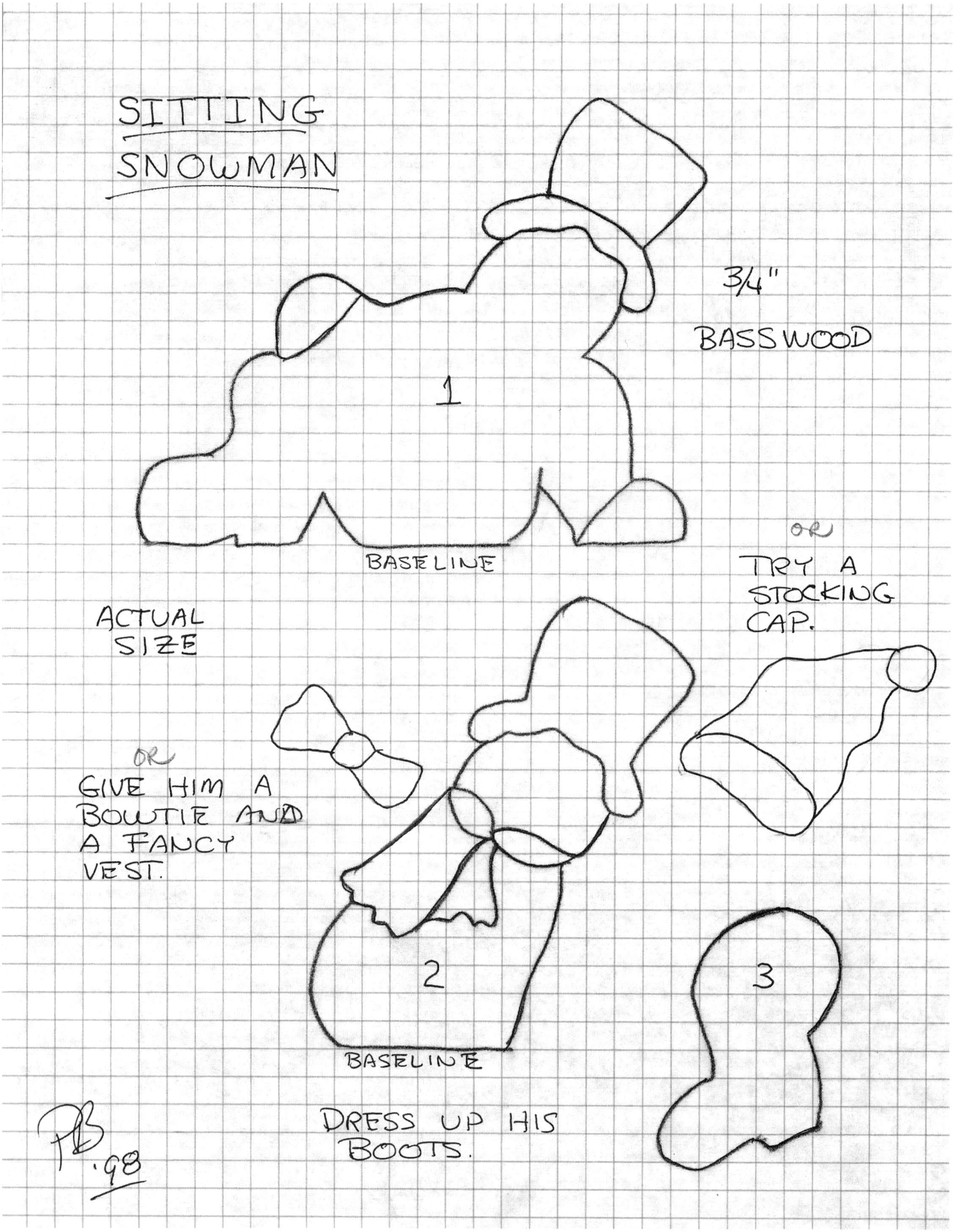
SITTING SNOWMAN
3/4" BASSWOOD
1
BASELINE
OR
TRY A STOCKING CAP.
ACTUAL SIZE
OR
GIVE HIM A BOWTIE AND A FANCY VEST.
2
BASELINE
3
DRESS UP HIS BOOTS.
PB '98

"Sitting Snowman"

The Snowman is semi-reclining and facing in the opposite direction from the bear. The pattern is in 3 pieces with piece 1 forming the bulk of the design. Piece 2 gives extra stock to the body and head of the piece. Piece 3 is simply his leg and boot. I didn't put the face on the pattern because that is for you to do on your own. His nose I made from a toothpick and Camille painted the rest. The baseline on this piece is wide and deep. On layer 1, his bottom, one hand, and one foot rest on the baseline. Part of layer 2 also rests on the baseline. Again, 2/3 of the carving sits on the shelf, while only 1/3 hangs over.

The first time I thought about carving snowmen I didn't think there would be much to it. Truthfully, there isn't much to getting the basic shape, but after that there can be many variations. As with the ghost designs in our Halloween carving book, snowmen turn out to be very versatile. Snowmen can be dressed in so many ways that it is not possible to discuss them all here. Because snowmen wear people's cast-offs, they really can wear anything that a person can. In many cases, they look better in the cast-offs than we once looked when the clothes were ours. So, go ahead and spice up your snowman carvings - add hats, vests, pants, boots, scarves, or whatever else you like.

This side view of the Sitting Snowman shows the depth of the carving plus the 2/3 to 1/3 ratio of the weight distribution. The carrot nose was made from a toothpick. You can really dress a snowman anyway you wish - the simple decoration on this one was done simply to keep costs down; yours doesn't have to be simple so "go for it."

The Sitting Snowman's posture is eye-catching as he leans to the side with his starburst held high.

The "Iceman" Snowman

In this carving, a snowman ice skater is caught doing the splits. We minimized the decorations while also altering the pose of the figure and attaching a sign. The result was enough decoration to catch the eye and create for a good design. The carving was done from a single piece of 3/4" basswood. Due to the design of the piece, it kind of breaks from the "shelf sitting" nature of the collection. I was able to save it though by adding the hanging sign, which helps to continue the overall theme. The baseline in this design runs the whole length of the snowman's outstretched legs and the weight of the sign is slight so there is no chance the snowman might be pulled off the shelf by the sign. When you use this design, you can add something other than a sign or change the sign I used. Another good sign would be "Snowman Collector," which would allow the piece to be used on a shelf where a snowman collection is displayed.

I also made the carrot nose for this snowman from a toothpick. Camille painted the remainder of the face, deciding on a traditional snowman face for this one's appearance made from lumps of coal. A snowman design can have pretty much any style face, including one that is much more realistic. "Anything goes," so give yourself the freedom to experiment.

This view of the "Iceman" Snowman shows that he is carved from a single piece of 3/4" stock.

This is the "Iceman" Snowman. He sits flat on the shelf with his sign hanging over the edge. This fellow was ice skating though snowmen are capable of all kinds of activities; you can experiment with different types of snowmen. Also, personalizing these pieces can be fun—a sign more meaningful to you would be a great modification.

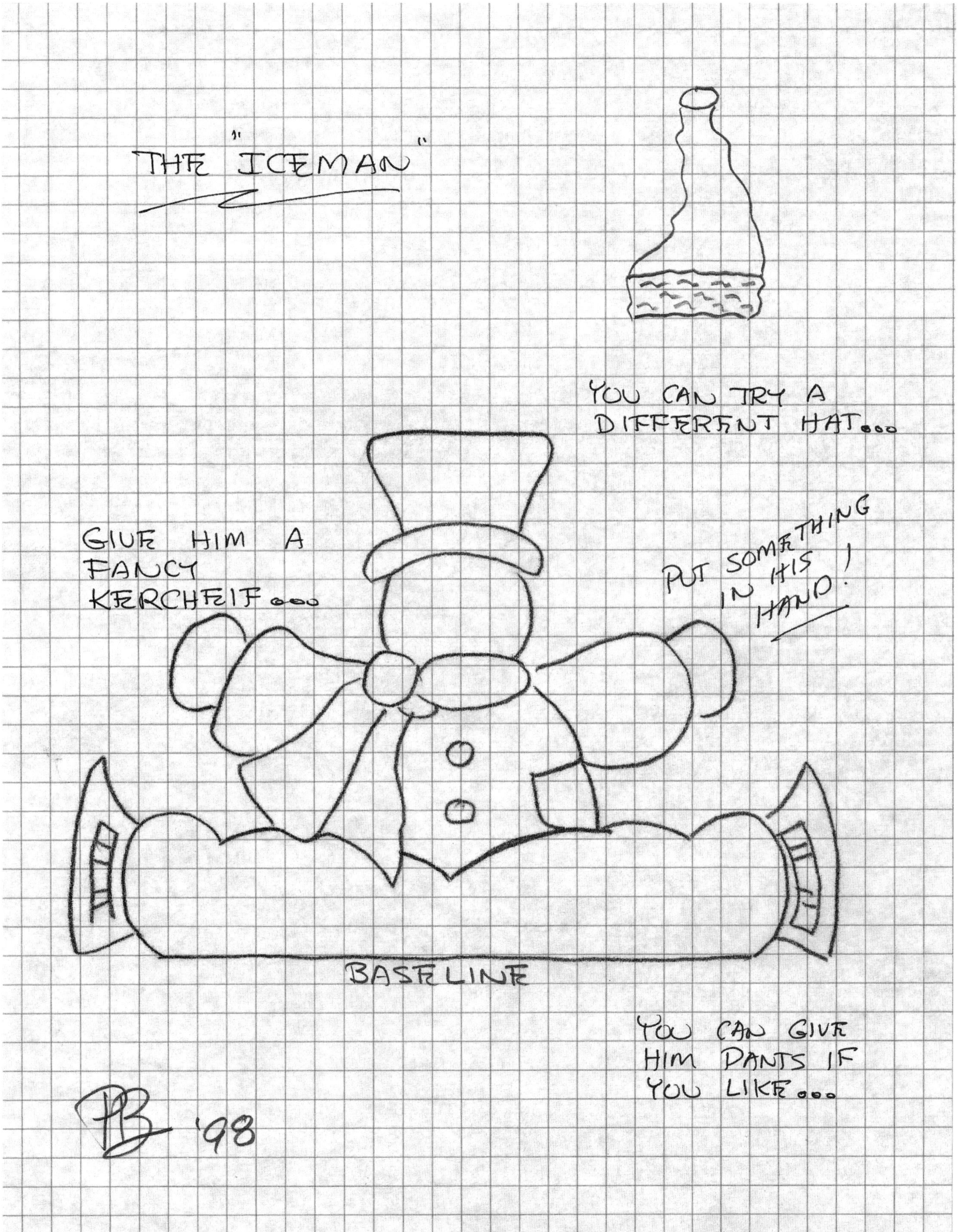
THE "ICEMAN"
YOU CAN TRY A
DIFFERNT HAT...
GIVE HIM A
FANCY
KERCHEIF...
PUT SOMETHING
IN HIS
HAND!
BASELINE
YOU CAN GIVE
HIM PANTS IF
YOU LIKE...
PB '98

"Hangover Santa"

Here Santa rests on his stomach with his head and arms out over the edge of the shelf and his beard hanging down. This piece is made from 4 separate cut-outs and there is a twist here where the boots are glued to the bottom of the coat in a different orientation so they sit on the shelf's surface - the bigger the boots, the more stable the piece. In this Santa, the baseline only exists on section 2, the coat. However, the boots give a lot of stability too. I was conservative with the size of the boots in the pattern, but you will notice in the picture of the piece that I actually made them quite a bit bigger. The face and beard were carved from 1/2" basswood, though 3/4" would work as well. I used 1/2" basswood because I felt the proportion would be better if the figure's beard and arms were from stock of that thickness. Make sure all the grain of pieces 2, 3, and 4 runs the same way - up through the beard is best. The tricky piece is the coat. Make sure you cut it out in the correct fashion so when glued together you won't have different grain directions to contend with. Because the boots are glued up in a different orientation, you may want to carve them before you glue them on.

Camille added a string of gold ornaments to the Santa to hang down past his beard. Almost anything that dangles would be great - maybe a string of stockings or even a sign. In painting the piece, she emphasized the coat with white highlights, applying them to give Santa's coat "roundness." Because the boots are at the back of the carving, they were kept black and simple. If you like, the design can be easily modified. Putting Santa's hat straight back overtop the middle of the coat would work, as would having a longer and more "dangly" hat going down one side.

This top view of the "Hangover" Santa shows the overall construction of the piece. Note how the boots are glued to the coat so they rest flat on the shelf to provide balance and how the face and beard were cut from 1/2" stock but 3/4" would also work.

This is the front view of the "Hangover" Santa. You can have fun with this style carving by modifying the length of the beard and by hanging other items from his hands

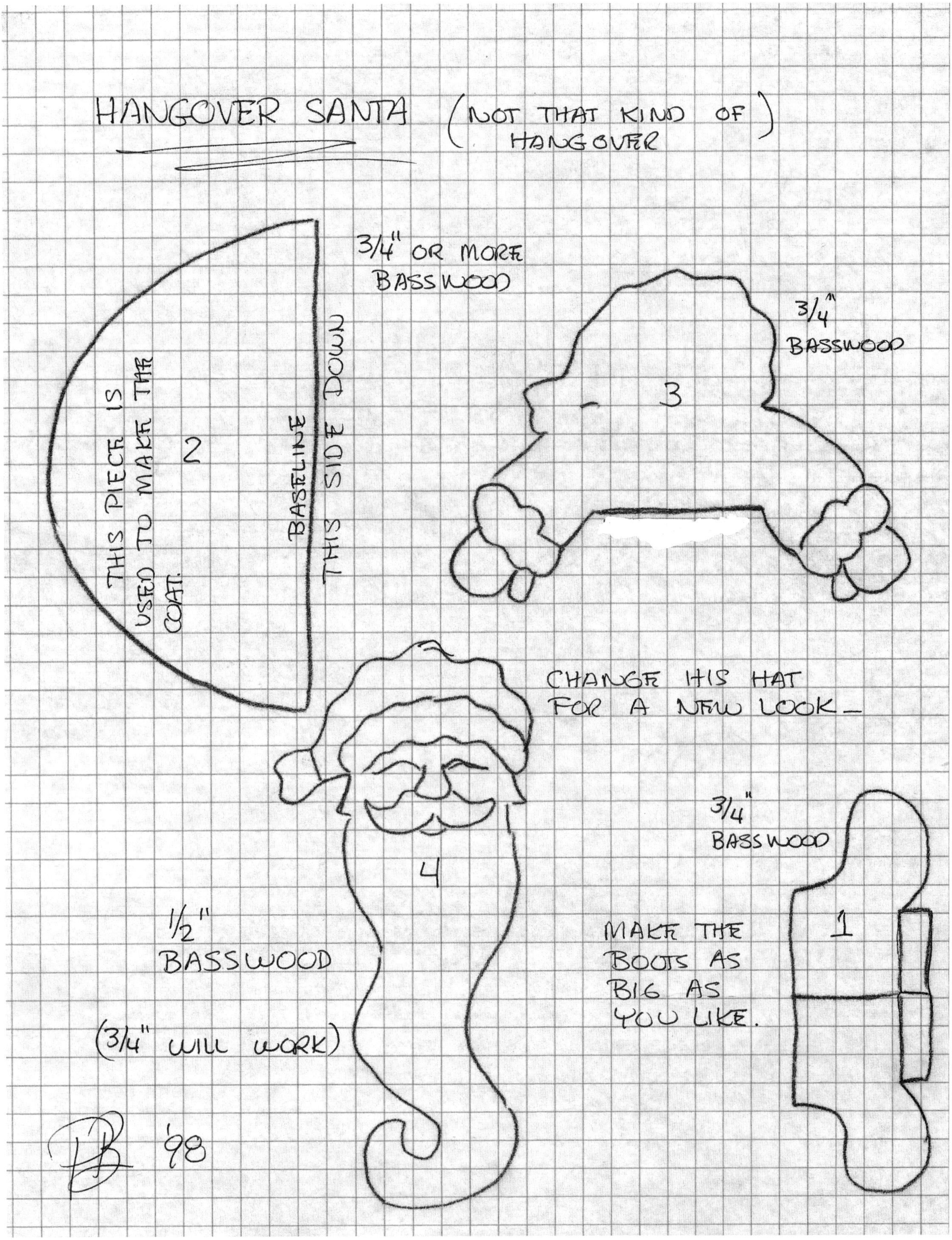
HANGOVER SANTA (NOT THAT KIND OF HANGOVER)
3/4" OR MORE BASSWOOD
THIS PIECE IS USED TO MAKE THE COAT.
2
BASELINE
THIS SIDE DOWN
3
3/4" BASSWOOD
CHANGE HIS HAT FOR A NEW LOOK –
4
1/2" BASSWOOD
(3/4" WILL WORK)
3/4" BASSWOOD
1
MAKE THE BOOTS AS BIG AS YOU LIKE.
'98

"Cooling His Heels" Santa

This Santa is pretty simple, but cute. The boots add a lot to the design, as do the stars he is holding. Santa has a unique flat topped hat, though other style hats would work as well. In the pattern, I added some balls on the toes of the boots, but didn't do them on the carving. I did the boots and legs from 1/2" basswood. Again, 3/4" could also be used. The baseline here exists on piece 1 and piece 2, so Santa is provided with quite a bit of sitting area. The 1/2" stock for the legs keeps the Santa from being unbalanced. I don't think 3/4" legs would have hurt - I was just conservative.

Camille painted this Santa conservatively also. He is mostly red suit and white beard. She highlighted his boots with polka dots, but stripes would work too. The starburst he holds adds whimsy.

This is a side view of the "Cooling his Heels" Santa.

This is the "Cooling His Heels" Santa. He can be dressed up in many ways. Adding something hanging from his other hand is an easy way to add to his appearance or a different hat would make an interesting change too.

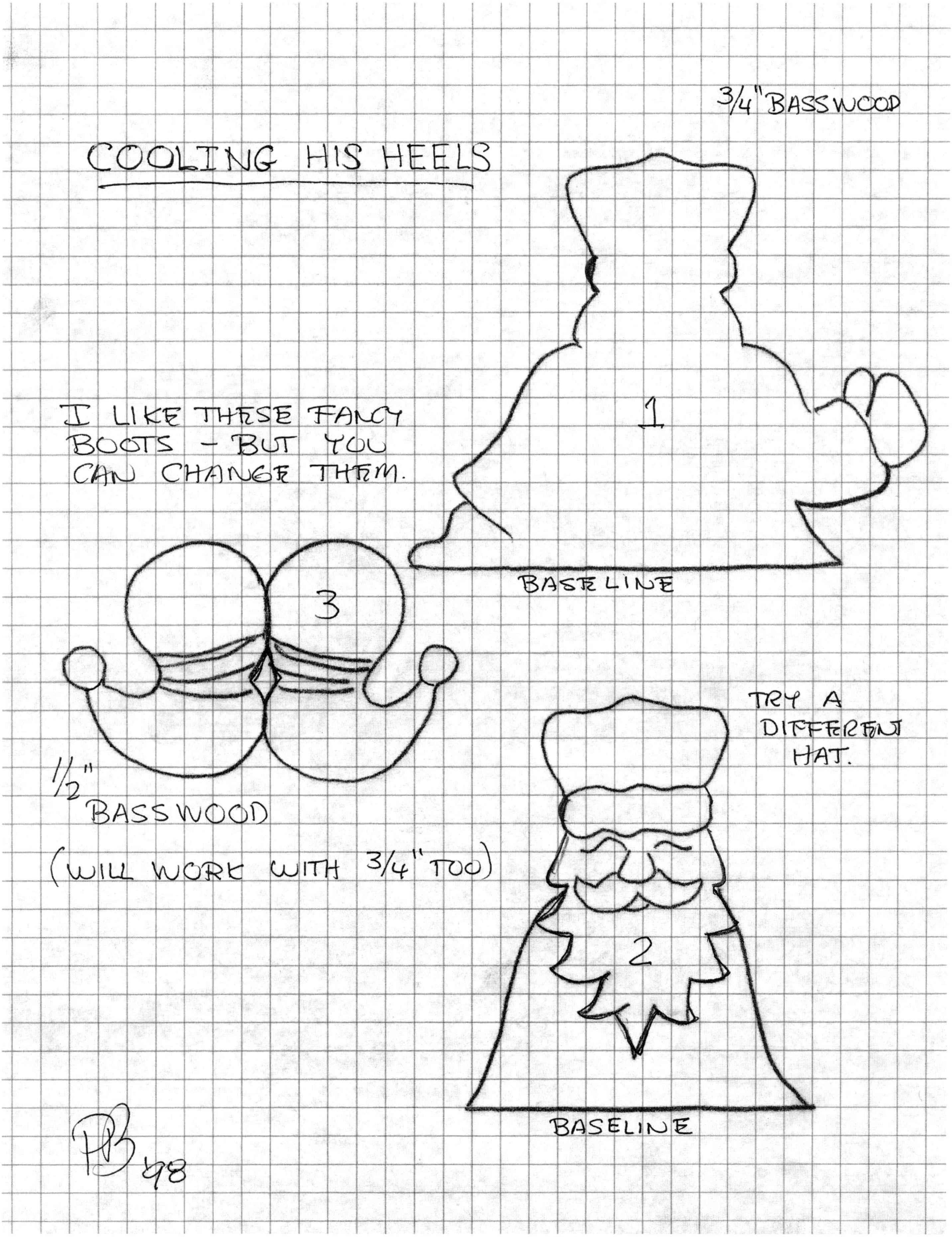
3/4" BASSWOOD
COOLING HIS HEELS
1
I LIKE THESE FANCY BOOTS - BUT YOU CAN CHANGE THEM.
BASELINE
3
TRY A DIFFERENT HAT.
1/2" BASSWOOD
(WILL WORK WITH 3/4" TOO)
2
BASELINE
PB 98

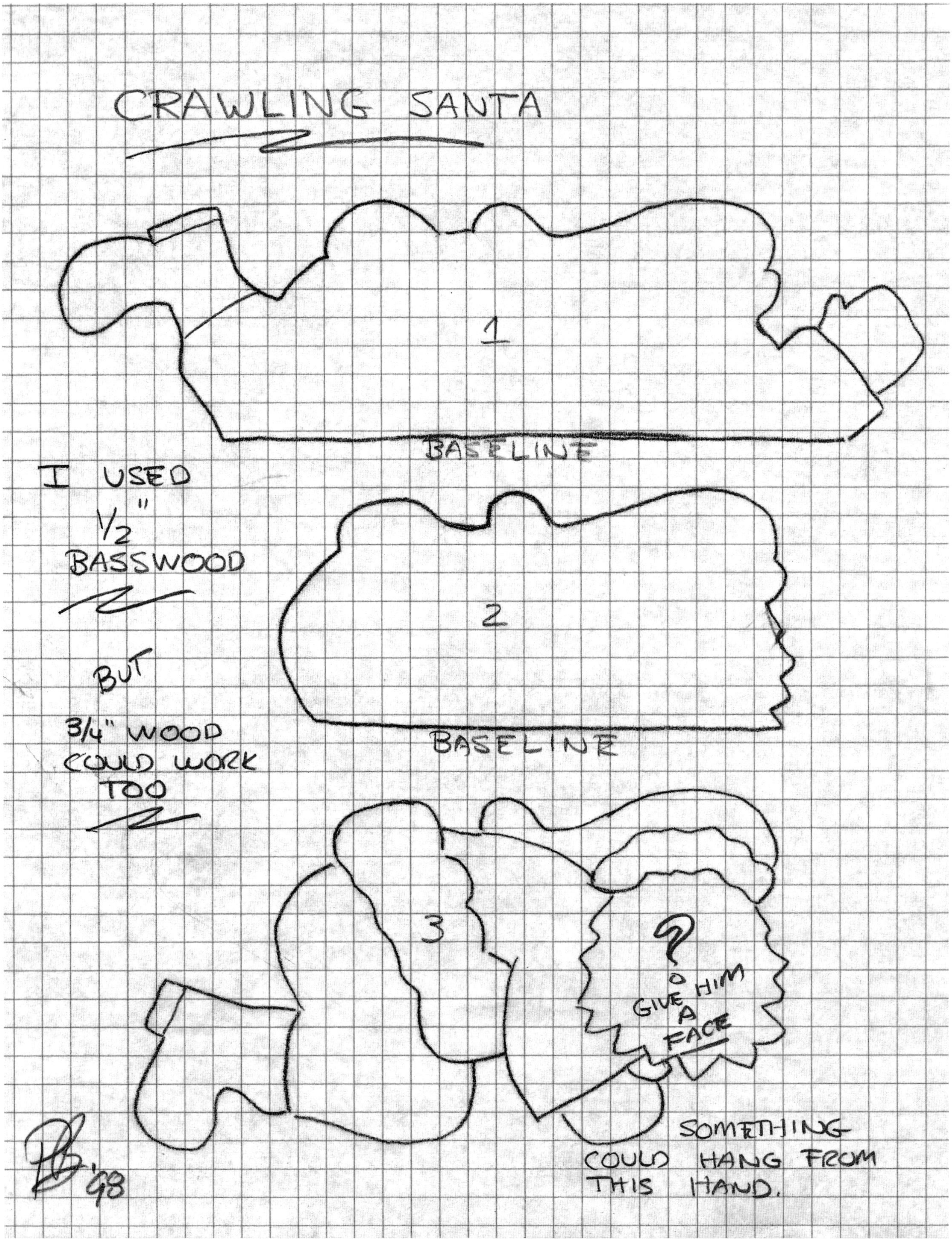
CRAWLING SANTA
1
BASELINE
I USED
1/2"
BASSWOOD
BUT
3/4" WOOD
COULD WORK
TOO
2
BASELINE
3
?
GIVE HIM A FACE
SOMETHING
COULD HANG FROM
THIS HAND.
'98

"Crawling Santa"

I guess this Santa could be crawling or swimming or who knows what. Whatever he is doing, he makes an interesting carving. The way he hangs down over the edge of the shelf is particularly appealing. This workpiece is glued up from 3 individual sections of 1/2" basswood, but he could work as well with 3/4" stock. Piece 1 forms the back of Santa plus his left leg and left arm. Piece 2 fills in the body area. Piece 3 provides the right arm, right leg, and the area on which to carve the face and some details. The baseline exists on piece 1 and 2. In my example, I ended up placing an additional piece of wood at the back to provide extra weight and stability to the piece. This piece I glued at right angles to the back of the Santa. You can see this added piece in the "top view" photo. If the carving were done all from 3/4" stock, it probably wouldn't need this counterbalance.

I didn't put a face on the pattern, so you can do it on your own. The sample designs I have provided for the Santa show the different mustache and eye styles possible. In its most simplistic form, a face can be done with the "nothing but nose" method, as I call it. Actually you carve the small round nose and whatever style mustache you choose, leaving the eye area smooth and just slightly rounded. On the eye area, you can then draw and paint the eyes very simply, using the two dot example I show. Carving eyes seems always to be a stumbling block for carvers, but I hope this simple method will help get you around that tough spot.

In keeping with the rest of the collection, Camille gave the "Crawling Santa" bright colors and polka dot highlights. I like the bell she gave him. The bends and twists in the bell wire give it a wild look, like Santa might be shaking the heck out of it. Again, the back is painted plain white.

This view shows this carving was glued up from 3 pieces of 1/2" basswood. Note the extra piece I glued on the back at a right angle to provide stability.

This is the front view of the "Crawling" Santa. I love the snappy bell Camille added.

"Standing Santa"

Santa is standing or more likely dancing since we can see his arms and feet in motion. I carved this Santa from one piece of 3/4" stock and originally intended him to be hanging from a rope or ribbon. The idea was that a piece of twine or ribbon would be pinned to the bookshelf to hang down through Santa's right hand. Something else would hang down from his left hand. Then, Santa would look like a mountain climber hanging from a rope off the edge of the shelf. After a while, we decided that driving a pin into a bookshelf might not be something a lot of customers would want to do, so we modified our design and provided a base for Santa to stand upon. In this example, I decided he would be standing on a chimney. The chimney is made from two pieces of 1/2" stock glued together at right angles. The overhanging part of the chimney gives this Santa the "shelf sitter" style it needs to be part of the collection. In your carving, feel free to find something else for Santa to stand upon or you may even wish to try my original idea and make your Santa hang down on a rope.

Camille dressed this Santa up with the bright colors and polka dots of the collection. I love the bow of stars she gave him; their textures, different sizes, and off-center positioning give the stars a great look. I made the eye sockets on this piece extra large so Camille would have room to create some more realistic eyes. Often I leave just a hint of an eye socket, so she must squeeze in some squinty eyes. In this case, Santa's eyes are wide open and clear - he is wide awake and having fun.

Refer to the back of the book for a page of design notes that shows you different possible Santa noses, mustaches, and beards. There are 5 different nose shapes, 6 different mustaches, and 4 different beards for you to check out. On the next page, I have drawn a simple Santa face using the same eyes in every case but using different noses, mustaches, and beards. Even with the face as the basic similarity, you can see the great variations that come out of this exercise. When carving this simple face, I would use the "nothing but nose" technique also located in the back of the book.

Another page of design notes shows the "same face with different mustache." Here, I used a better looking basic set of eyes and a set nose, and varied only the mustache. Again, you can see the differences, even with the great similarity of the faces.

On the page "six faces - six different beards," I mixed up mustaches and beards to build some Santa faces for you. Look at them closely. Which do you like best? Which do you not like? Can you duplicate them yourself?

This "Standing Santa" has a great bow of hearts, which creates the illusion of movement. While he doesn't actually hang over the edge, the chimney base I made for him does. This carving can also be made to hang from a string or ribbon.

The side view shows that this Santa (excluding the chimney) was done from a single piece of 3/4" stock. I made the chimney from two pieces of 1/2" stock glued together at right angles.

STANDING SANTA

GIVE HIM A FACE

3/4" BASSWOOD

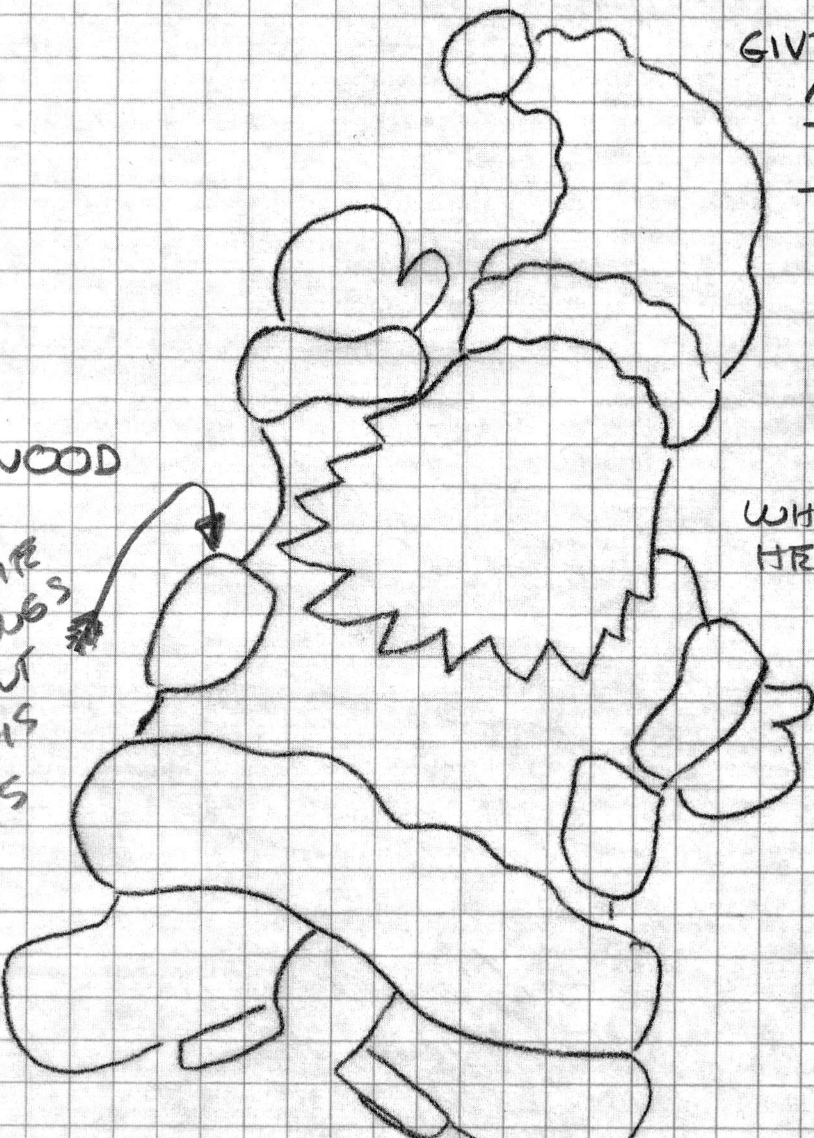

WHAT IS HE HOLDING?

MAKE SOME CUTE THINGS COME OUT OF HIS POCKETS

WHAT IS HE STANDING ON?

FIGURE OUT SOMETHING FUN FOR HIM TO STAND ON - OR USE MY CHIMNEY IDEA

'98

Five Faces For Santa

In these examples, I drew one outline of a face with a beard and a hat then copied it five times so that the basic size and shape of Santa's face was exactly the same in every case. If you study these five faces, you can see the different facial elements. Look at the noses, the eye styles, and particularly the mustache styles. I tried to place the face in roughly the same position on the drawing; however, moving the face location up or down also would have dramatic effects on the outcome.

The middle face of the three on the right is the one that I call "nothing but nose." In this case, you would carve away from the nose area leaving a teardrop shape nose plus a mustache hanging down. You can then draw the eyes in as nothing but dots; note how the placement of the eyes changes the face quite a bit. The eyes I did are just dots and they are close to the nose giving Santa a kind of surprised look. If you look at the top one of the three Santas you see that those eyes are also just dots, but the face has a different look. This difference is mainly due to the little lines under the eyes, which indicate cheeks, and the size and placement of the features; they are bigger and the eyes are farther out from the nose.

When you design your faces, if you like you can try to achieve a certain look or feel or you can just draw the facial elements onto the carving and see what happens. Sometimes just "hacking away" at the face will produce a cute look.

This Santa shows how a different type of base makes a great addition. Here I made a small "Mantle" with Christmas stockings hanging from it. This was made from two pieces of 1/2" stock glued together at right angles.

FIVE FACES FOR SANTA
SQUINTY EYES
DROOPY MUSTACHE
ROUND EYES
BIG "STASH"
BEADY EYES
DROOPY "STASH"
OPEN EYES
HAPPY UP MUSTACHE
HAPPY "UP" MUSTACHE
HAPPY EYES
'98

PRACTICE PIECES

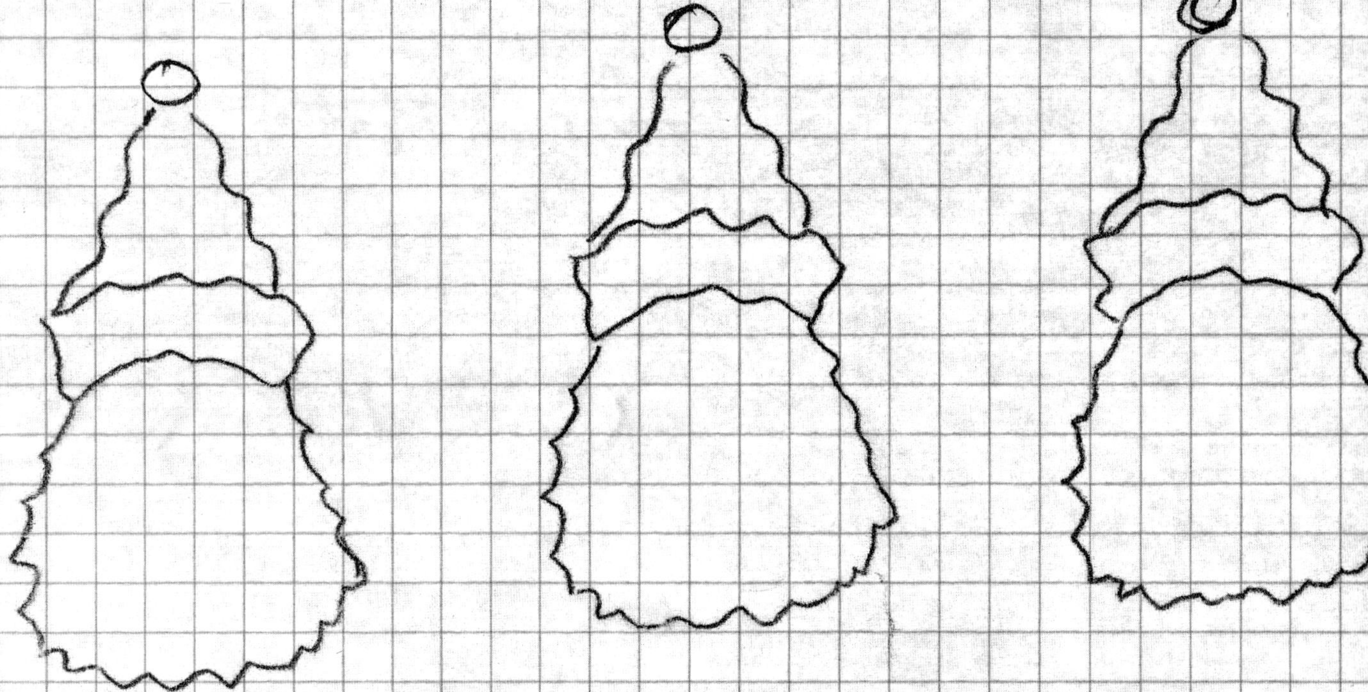

GO AHEAD AND PUT SOME FACES ON THESE SANTA HEADS.

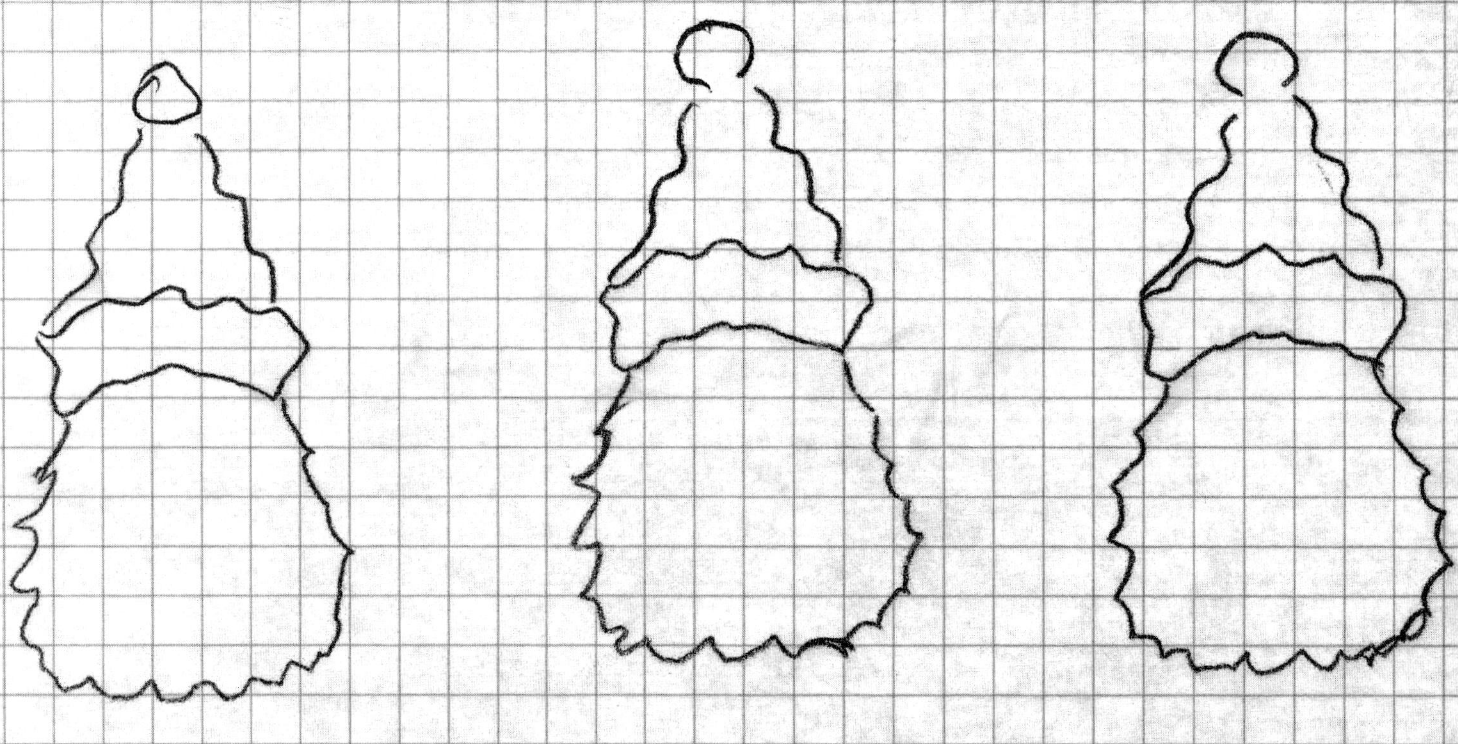

You might benefit from doing the same exercise that I did with the five faces. Draw one outline and then use carbon paper to make several copies of the blank face or photo copy the drawing several times. When you have all the blank faces, go ahead and try different eyes, mustaches, mouths, etc. Once you've done that, then try adding different beard styles. You know what - I've saved you the trouble of drawing the basic outlines and have provided you a worksheet with 6 blank faces for you to fill in. Have at it!

Variations

I have provided some additional drawings that are variations on the patterns previously presented. In these drawings, you can see how I draw the complete project with the exclusion of the breakdown into sections - you can decide these for yourself.

The two bears are variations on the pattern I provided. These two are facing what would be the front of the bookshelf. Both of these have faces that are full frontal and, therefore, need to be carved to some level of detail. Look at the difference in the hats; one disappears, while one dominates the piece. Note also how the fishing bear's eyes are looking toward his fish, which causes your eyes to look at the fish too.

In the Santa variations, I show some designs and design modifications that I didn't use. The bigger Santa is a variation of the "Standing Santa" pattern in which I spread the legs and modified the hat for a slightly different look. The "Crawling Santa" shows a slightly different position for his hanging leg and he is slightly elongated for a different look. The little Santa with the big hat shows how the simple change of emphasizing the hat can make a different carving. The little Santa with his arms raised could make anything a shelf piece or an ornament depending on what he is doing with his upraised arms. From each of these design variations, you can see how even the smallest modifications can make a difference in the overall look and feel of a piece. Give it a try and do your own design. (see next page for variations)

HEAD FACES "FORWARD"

VARIATIONS

BIG HAT

'98

VARIATIONS
DB '98
PUT THINGS IN HIS POCKETS.
WHAT GOES HERE
BIG HAT
SMALL SANTA

Chapter Three
Carving the Stocking Santa

This Santa has an appealing design because of his size and his great hat. I wanted this Santa to be extra fat and also for it to have a carved back, so I put one more piece into the glue up. This Santa is glued up from 5 layers of 3/4" with 4 and 5 being identical. Layer 1 provides the back and the arms for Santa. Layer 2 provides more stock and the top half of the face. Layer 3 provides more belly and the lower half of the face. In the photos, you can see the glue lines that separate the different parts. He makes a neat workpiece when glued up and ready to carve - looks inviting doesn't it?

The pattern (found on page 53 & 54) indicates the beard position on layer 3, but in reality you need to wait until you have glued the legs onto the front of layer 3 before you indicate where the beard goes. You can dowel the legs onto layer 3 when you glue it - this will add strength. I just glued the two legs directly to layer 3 without dowels and clamped the whole thing in a vise for the night. I was careful when carving the legs later though just in case they might pop off when I exerted pressure on my knife.

To begin the carving, I mounted the piece to a carving arm using a carver's screw. Because of his legs, I was not able to rotate the piece to the side or backward. Eventually, I had to remove the piece and hold it while I carved. Most of the heavy "whacking" was needed to get the front shaped up and once that was done I was comfortable with taking the piece off the carving arm and holding the piece for the rest of the carving.

For variations, you can easily modify Santa's arm position and certainly the legs can be changed easily. Just changing the position of the legs can give you a different look that you might like. Can you figure out how to make legs that cross in front of Santa? How about leaning his knees into the center or out from the center so his legs don't go straight up and down? Go ahead and play with the pattern before you begin.

This is the glued up workpiece for the fat Santa. Her he is sitting on the end of a carving arm to show his dangling legs.

de view of glued up workpiece.

Back view with piece tilted.

Bottom view of piece. The hole is to accommodate the carver's screw.

Inserting the carver's screw. No, he doesn't feel any pain.

Note how the glued up piece is "stepped" so that there is extra wood for a belly, beard, and lower mustache. I started carving on the body using shallow "U" gouges. Secure the piece on the carver's arm so that the "heavy hitting" can be done.

Chips are starting to fly from the beard area. With the piece secured on the arm I can hack away and remove the bigger chips.

Working with a shallow "U" gouge shape back the beard area.

Shape up the sides of the body.

Go slowly as you work. You will be "peeling the onion" in layers so there is no need to take all the wood away on the first pass. I always work the piece over in layers to avoid going too far in one spot and ruining the carving.

Work the other side of the body for a while. It is important to keep moving around the piece and unpeeling the layers. Working too long on one spot can throw off the balance of the piece.

Shape up the beard.

Round the knees a little.

Round the hat using a shallow "U" gouge.

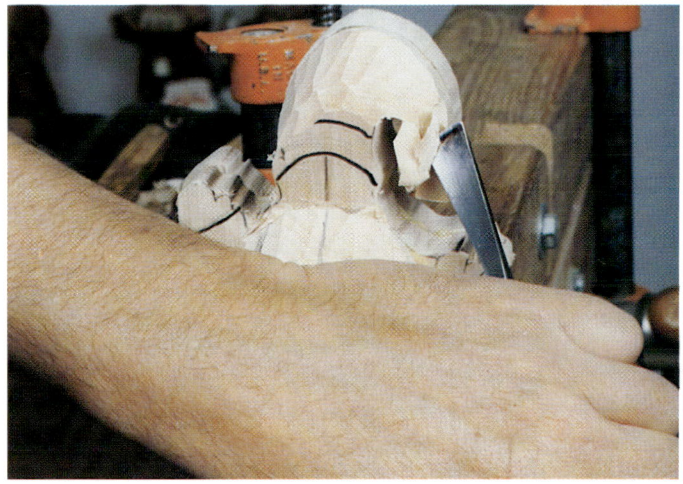
Work the side of the hat too.

Continue to round the hat and lean it back.

Use a "U" gouge to outline the beard area.

More hat work.

Outline the other side of the beard.

Remove wood from outside the beard area.

Shape the beard all the way down to the knees.

To get between the knees, shape the beard using a smaller "U" gouge.

Start shaping Santa's right arm (the one on your left). The arm is quite a bit thicker than you want it. But go slowly and don't overdo it. You will be back again.

Continue to shape the arm.

Define the line between the body and the arm.

More arm shaping.

Define the line between the arm and the body.

Shift over to the other side to keep the piece in balance. Use the "eyeball" method to judge when you should shift sides.

Start shaping the other arm. Note that the arm is double the thickness of 3/4" stock, but don't go too fast. You can always come back.

Shape up the lower side of the body.

Shape the arm.

Recut the arm line and keep moving the arm back.

I redrew the lines to mark the hat.You will need to redraw your guidelines to keep on track.

Round the "inside" of the hat. Be careful of the grain here.

Invert a "U" gouge to cut a stop cut into the line marking the bottom of the hat.

Push the hat back a little.

Run up to the stop cut and remove wood from the upper face area.

Cut the line deeper.

Shape the hat.

Shape the face. Because you have a long way to go, just try to keep the face rounded a little at this point - don't worry about facial features.

Yes, you want to cut back here a little. You will redraw the lines later.

Shape the hat above the upper line. This will define the "fur" around the stocking cap.

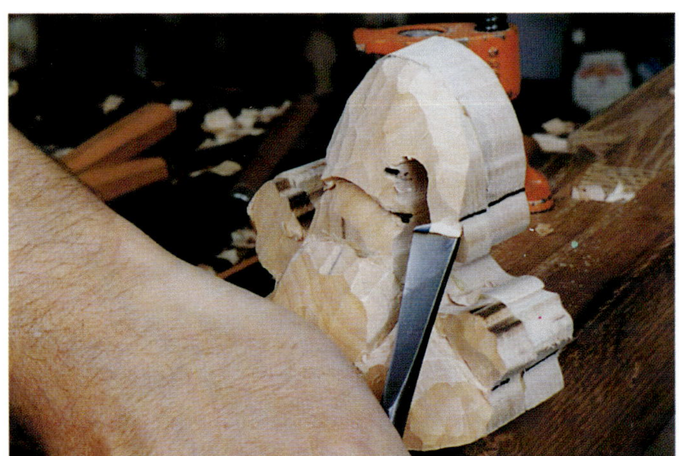

Shape the tassel end of the hat back some more.

Shape the hat back more.

Push the arm back some more. You can see where I am cutting in relation to the glue line between the two pieces of the arm.

Cut down on the front of the hat "fur" area. This will let more light hit the face.

Redraw the face onto the piece. You can put on the piece any face you want. Looking back at all the design notes may help you to decide the expression you will use.

Use a small "U" gouge to put a stop cut at the bottom of the nose.

Also use a small "U" gouge to remove the wood below the nose.

Use a small "U" gouge to put a stop cut at the top of the mustache.

Use a small "V" gouge or a knife to outline the sides of the nose.

To separate the top of the mustache from the cheek, use a small "U" gouge and cut down to the stop cut.

Here you can see the nose outlined on the bottom and sides. This is the way to approach doing the "nothing but nose" face I described earlier in the chapter two.

Use a small "U" gouge to put a stop cut along the top of the eye socket. Don't go too deep. More will be done later.

Use a small "U" gouge to remove the wood from the eye socket.

Cut the stop cut above the other eye and then remove the wood from the socket. At this point, my wife wandered into the background of the shot, squealed when the flash went off, and then bolted.

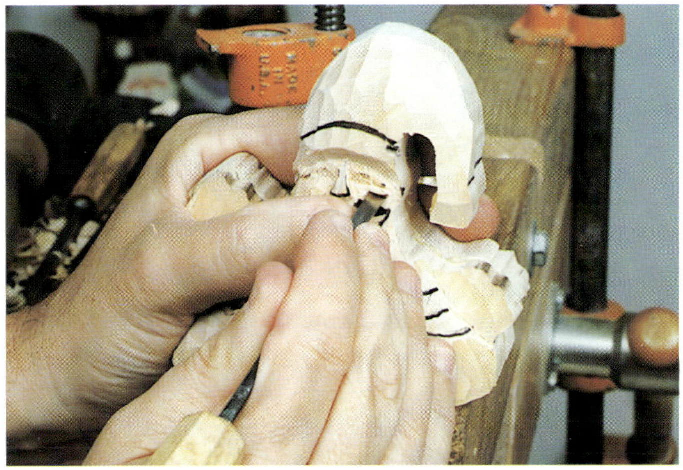

Clean up the eye area.

Use a "U" gouge to put a stop cut under the mustache.

Cut up to the stop cut and remove wood from the beard below the mustache.

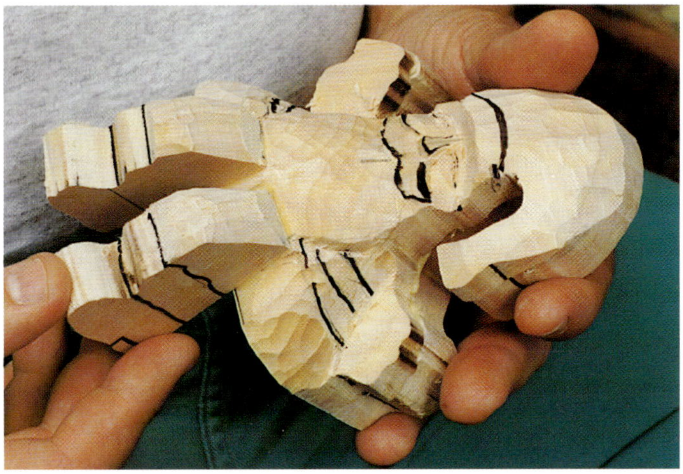

I have removed the piece from the carver's arm and will hold it from here on. The three lines on the side of the body define the upper and lower edge of the belt and the top edge of the fur trim that will decorate the bottom of the coat.

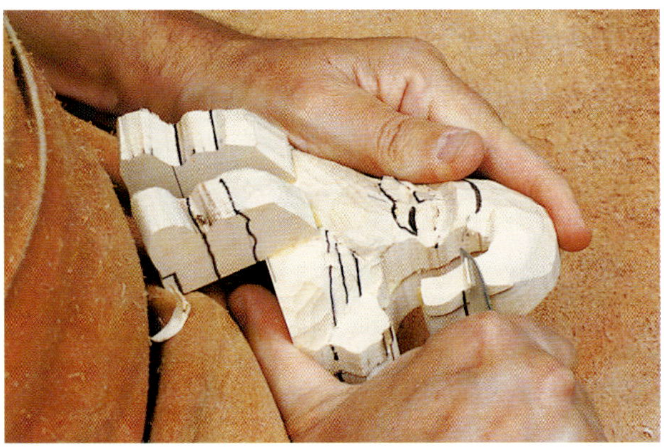

Use a knife to shape the tassel end of the hat. The brown garment in the photo is a leather apron I wear to keep from sticking myself in the leg (or worse).

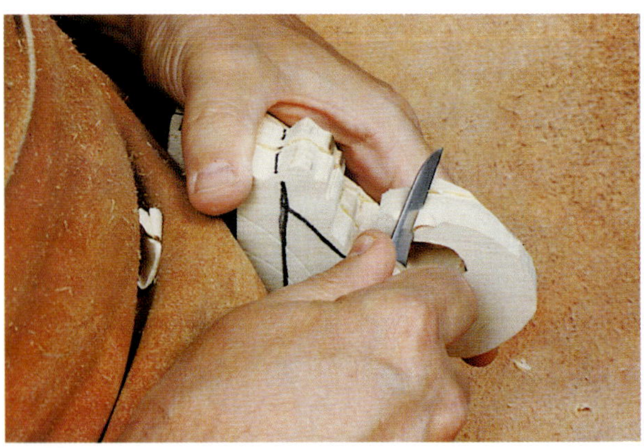

Start shaping the back of the hat.

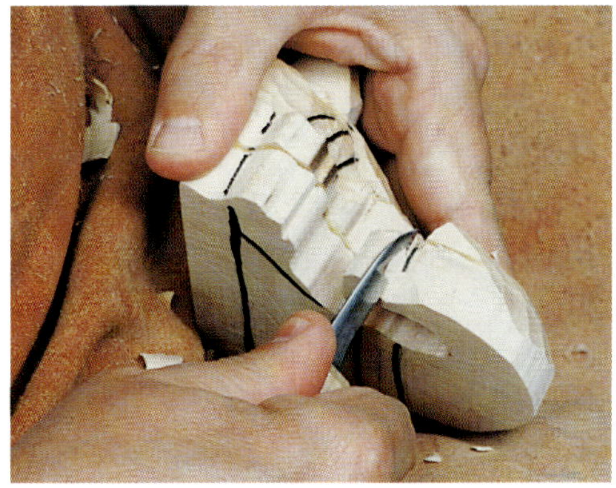

Carve the line between the hat and the tassel.

Shape the tassel.

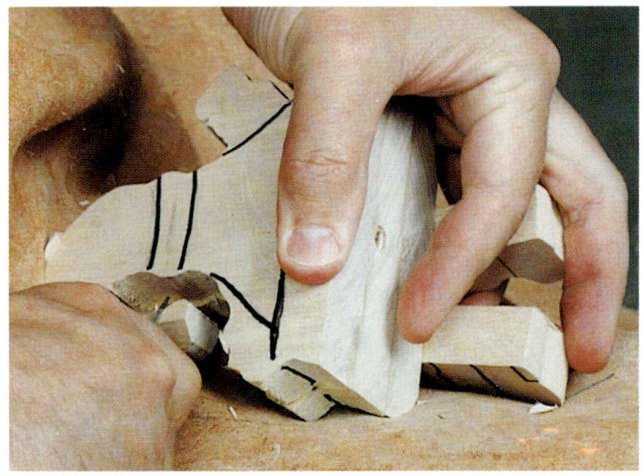

Hat work.

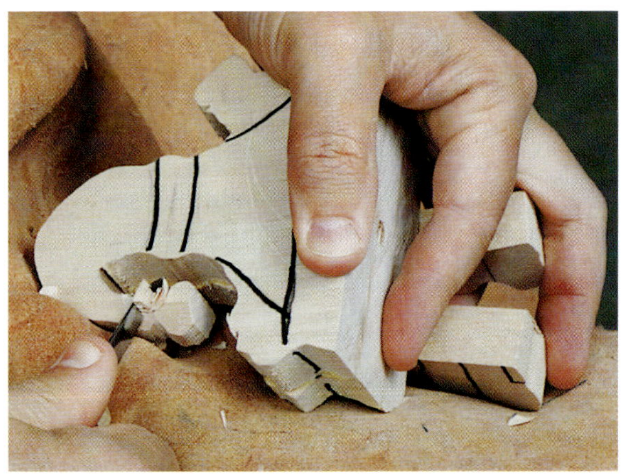

Shape the hat.

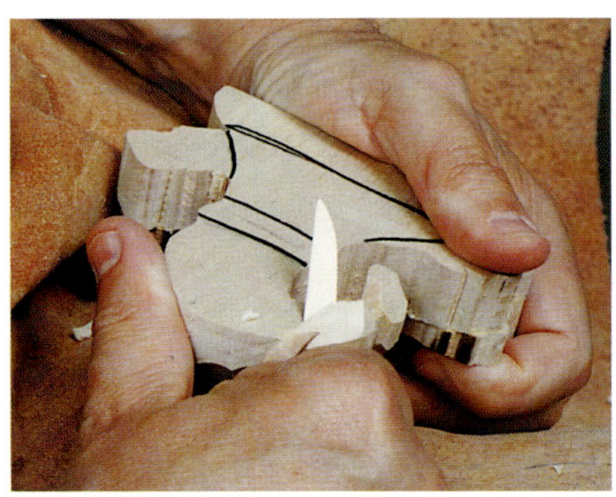

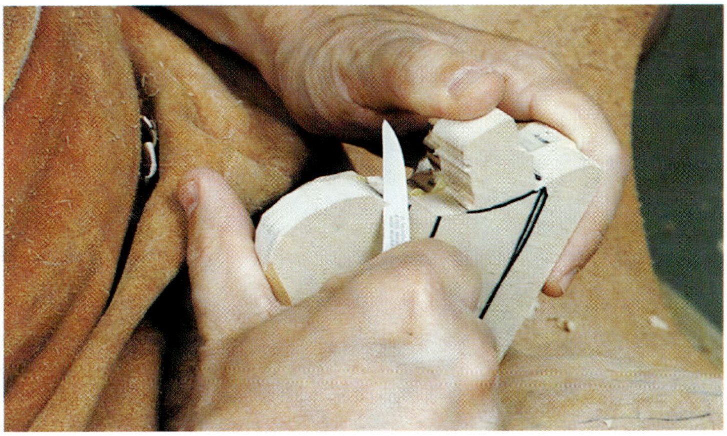

More hat work.

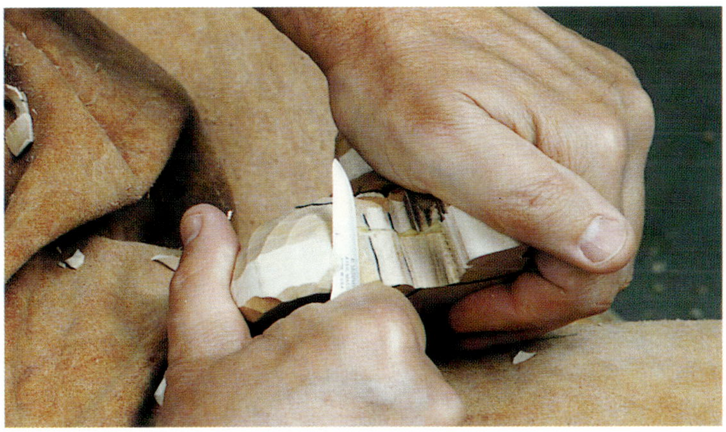

Start shaping the top of the hat.

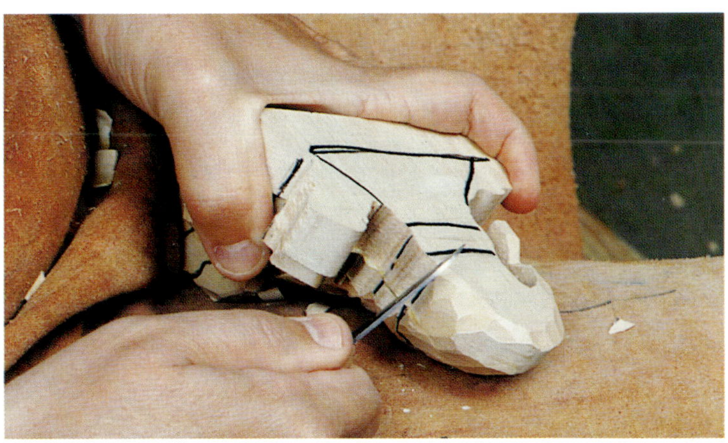

Cut the line between the hat and the fur trim at the bottom of the hat.

Define this line and continue shaping the hat.

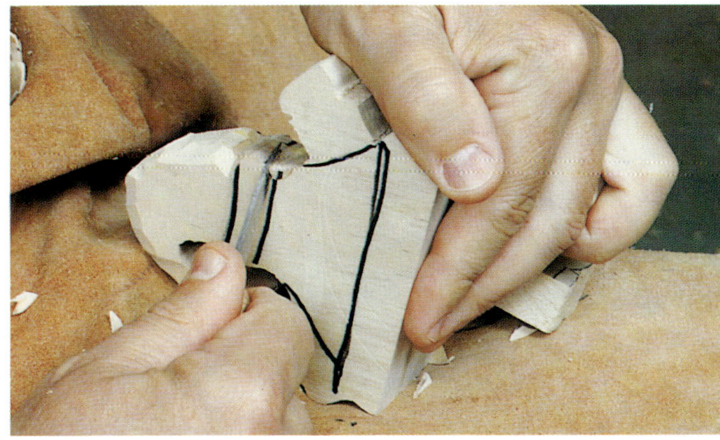

Cut the defining lines.

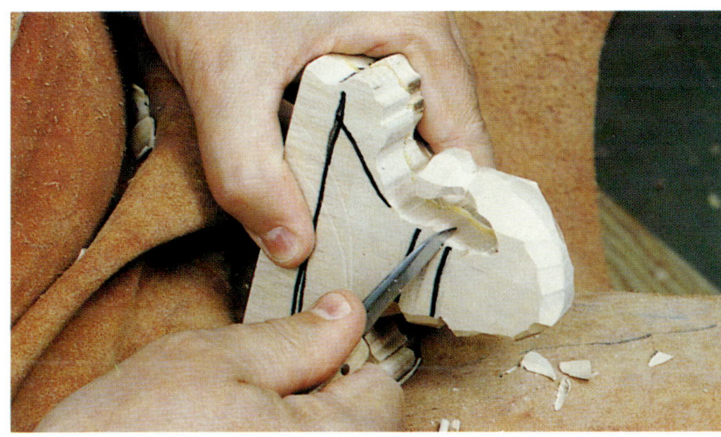

Make up and down cuts into the line to mark it better.

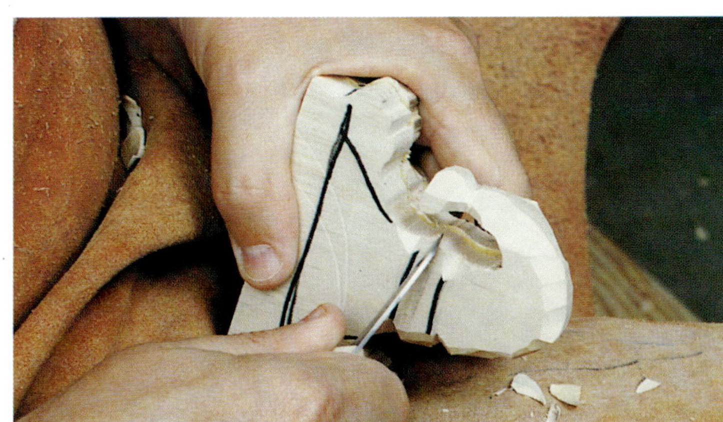

Cut the line all the way around the hat.

Go around to the front of the hat.

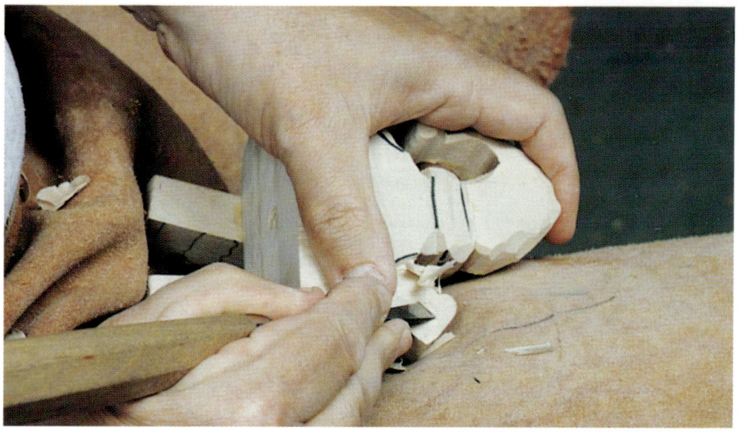

Shape the back of the arm.

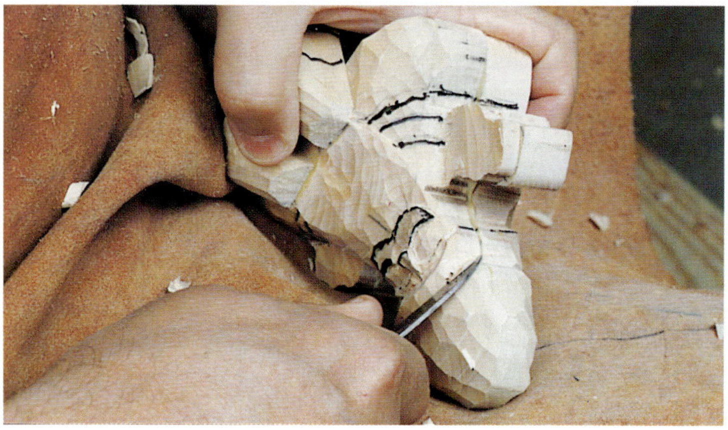

More hat work.

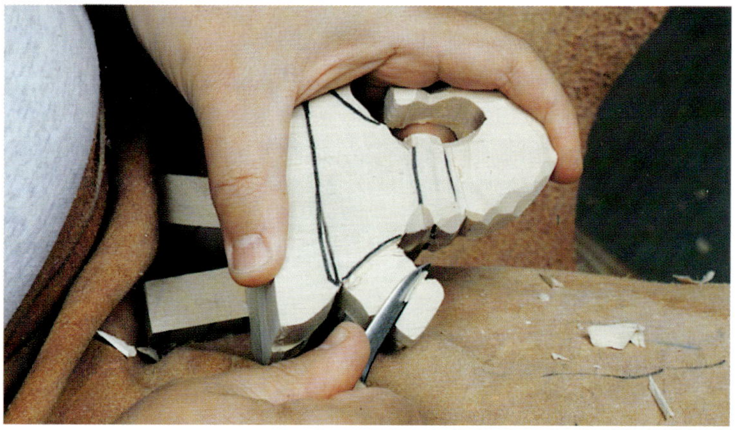

Shape the back of the hand.

Shape the fur trim.

Recut the line deeper.

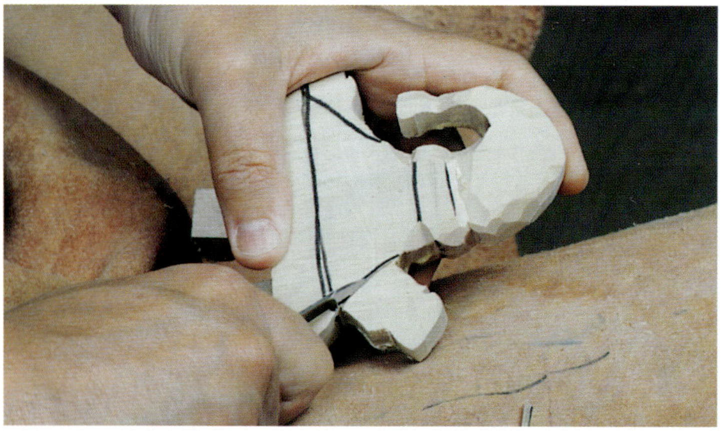

Cut the line between the back of the arm and the back of the body.

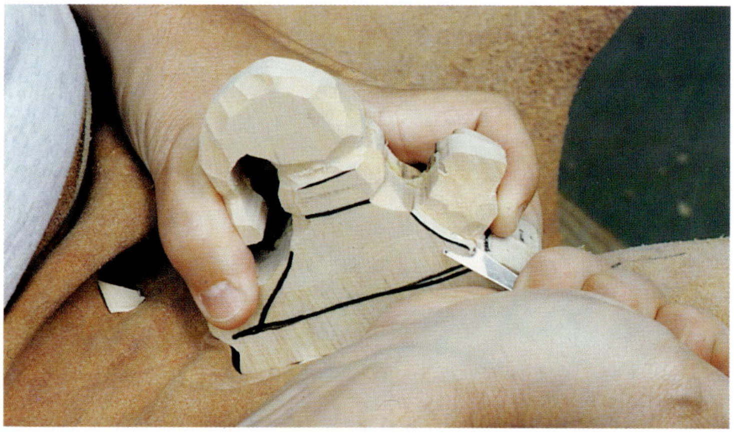

Shape the back of the body.

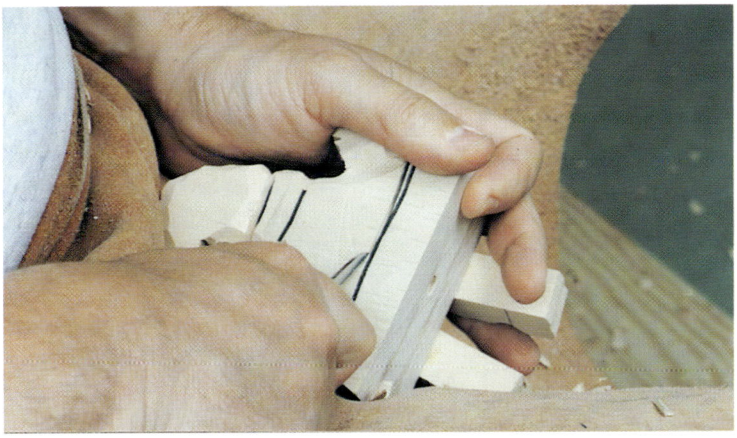

Make a stop cut along the line that is the top of the "fur" trim on the coat.

Use a gouge to remove wood into the stop cut and shape the body.

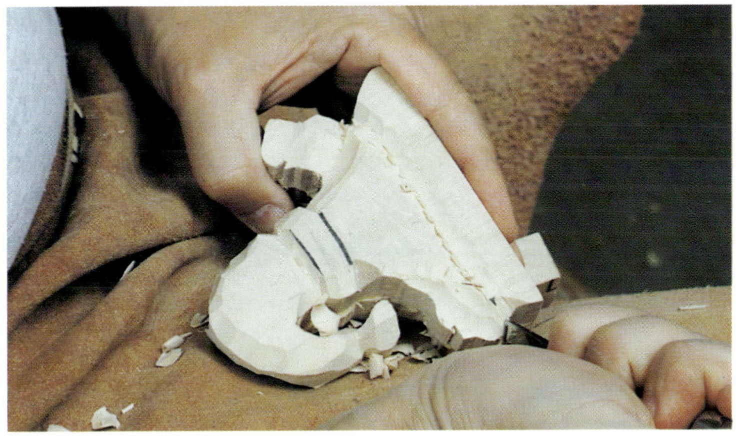

Shape the back of the arm.

Use a gouge to remove wood first from above and then from below the stop cut.

Shape the back of the hat.

Cut the line between the other arm and the back of the coat.

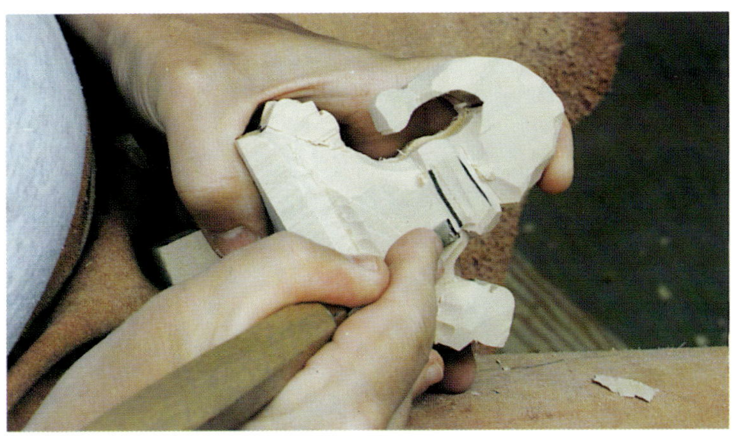

Shape the line at the bottom of the hat.

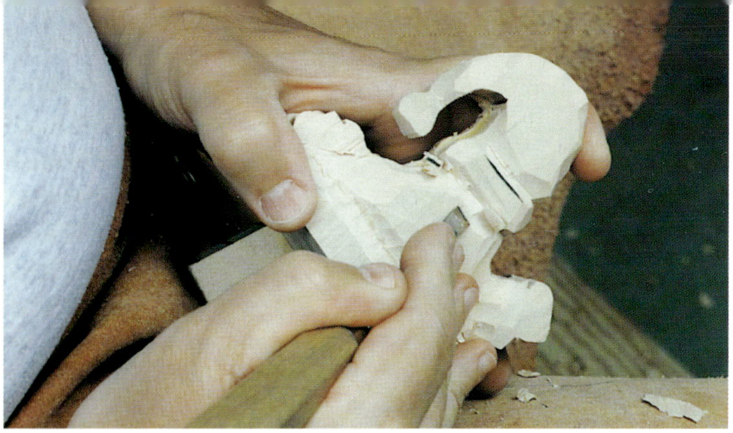

Shape the hair up to the bottom of the hat.

Here, I am using a "U" gouge turned sideways to put a cut along the side of the nose.

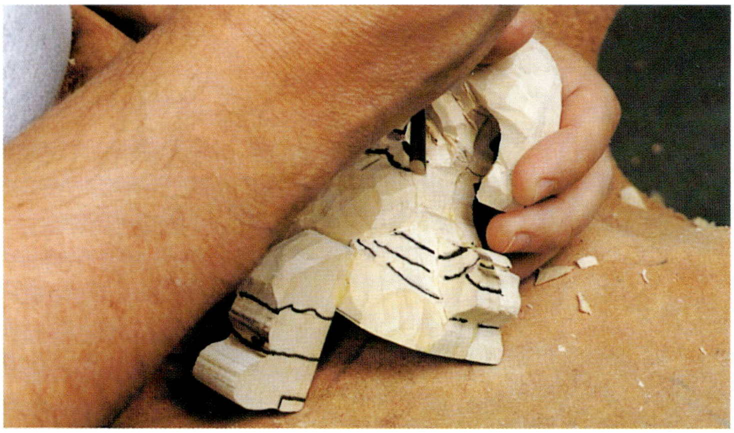

Put a stop cut along the bottom of the mustache.

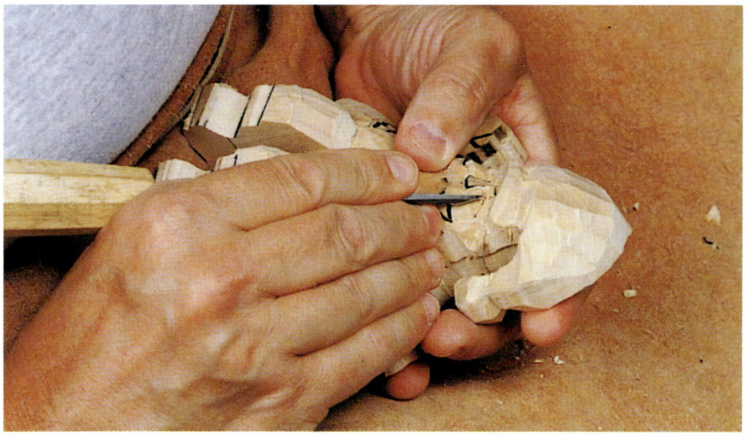

Remove a small amount of wood from the side of the nose to emphasize the nose more.

Remove the wood from below the mustache.

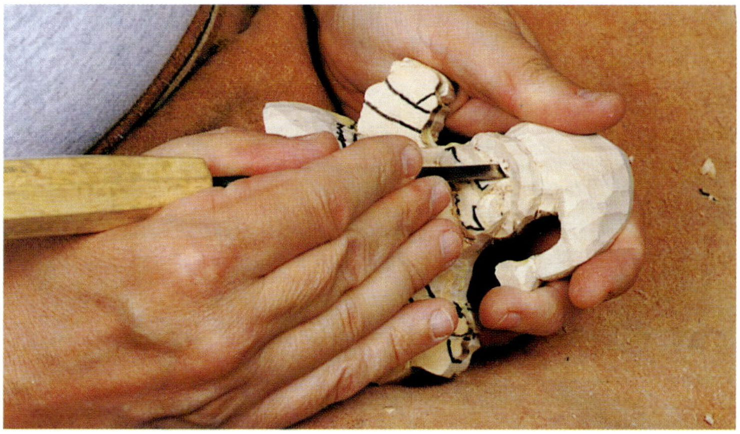

Shape the face more. Now you are doing another layer of onion peeling. Go slowly and just take a little at a time.

Push back the beard far enough so the mustache sticks out above it.

Here is the way the piece should look at this point. There's still work to be done but the overall face and shape have been decided.

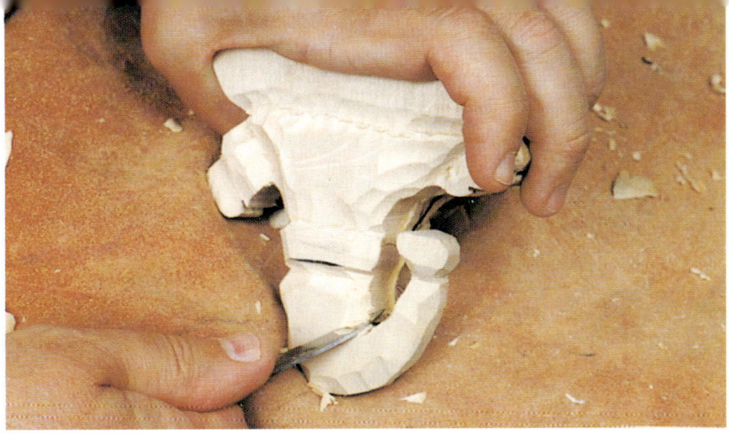

Go back to shaping the rear of the hat.

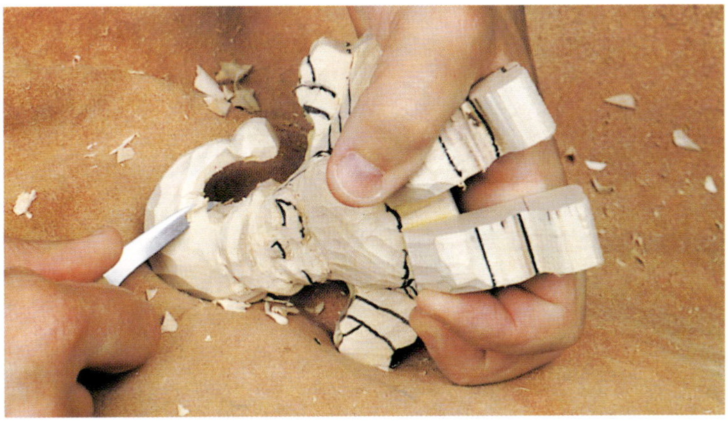

Shape the inside of the hat's folds. As the hat bends over to the side, it makes a series of folds - you want to give the illusion of these cloth folds.

Outline the beard once more. This will lead to an additional "peeling". Cut away some more wood from outside the beard.

Outline the other side of the beard by cutting away some wood from outside the beard.

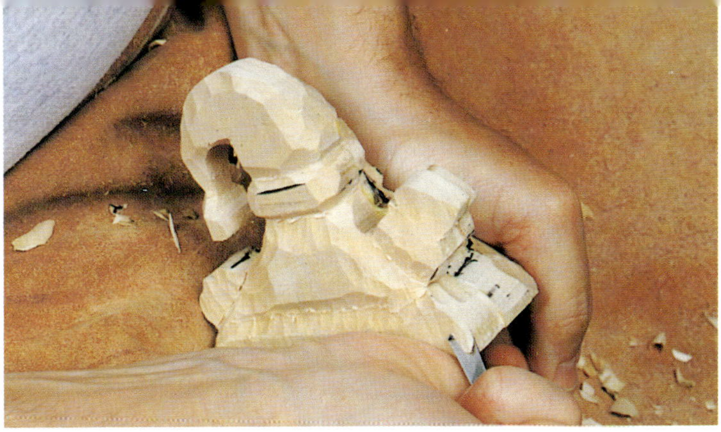

Shape the remaining areas of the body.

Make a stop cut between the legs where you want the bottom of the beard to be.

Cut away up the stop cut. This will define the bottom of the beard.

Shape any remaining areas along the bottom of the fur to get the shape you want. Remember the fur trim can be uneven. It doesn't need to be perfectly round.

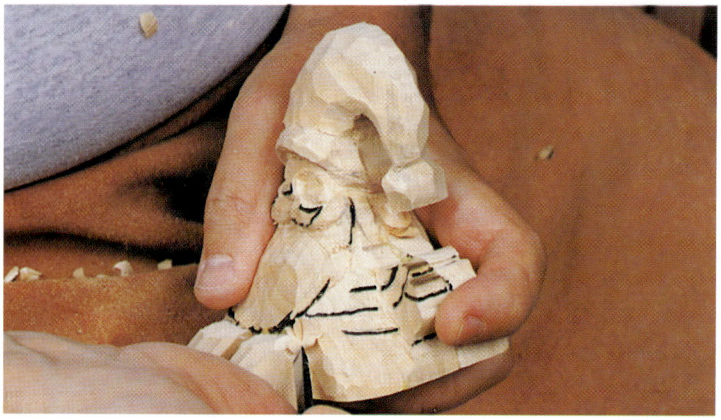

Shape the body up to the bottom of the beard. Shape the side of the leg a little too.

More onion peeling on the back of the hat. You will know when you get it to look the way you want.

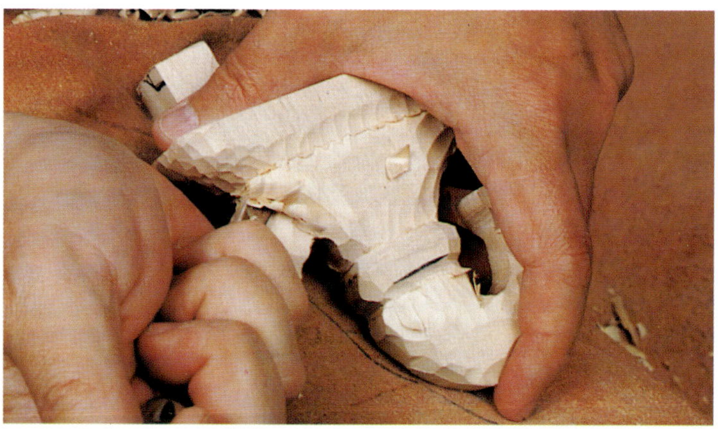

More defining of the bottom of the coat/top of the fur trim.

Shape the hands more. The lines mark the fur cuff that I will have on the coat.

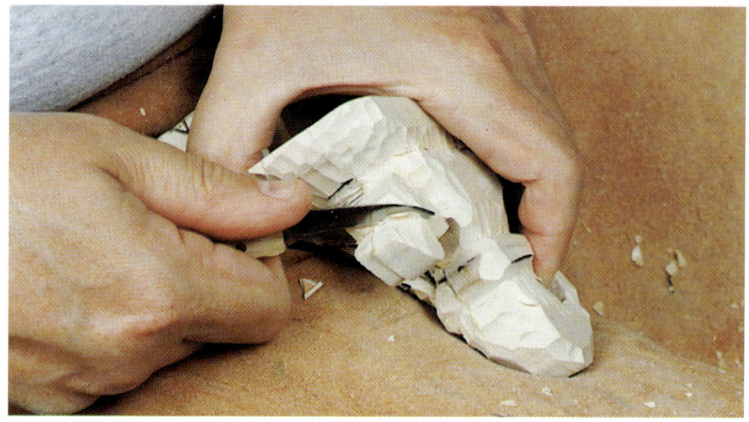

Shape the back of the hands.

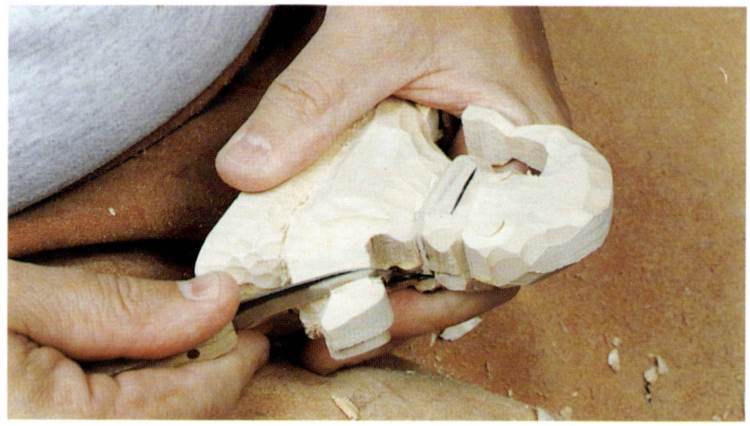

You can see the glue line on the hand in this shot.

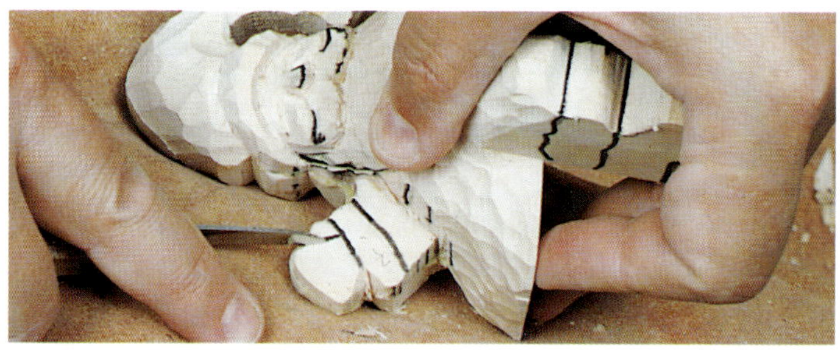

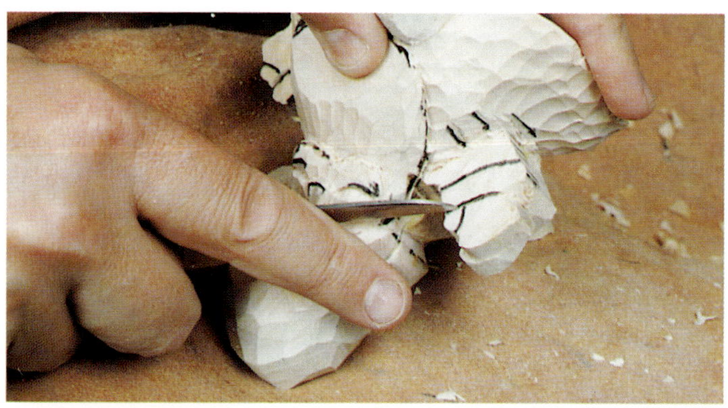

Cut the line that separates the thumb from the hand, the fur cuff from the hand, and the fur cuff from the coat.

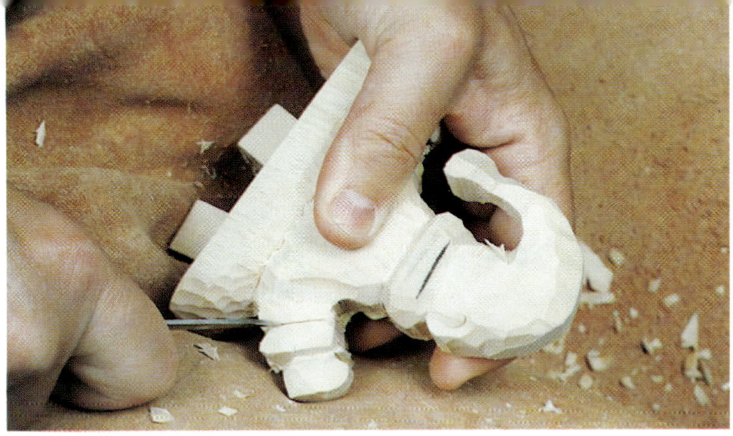

Cut the fur cuff lines at the back of the coat.

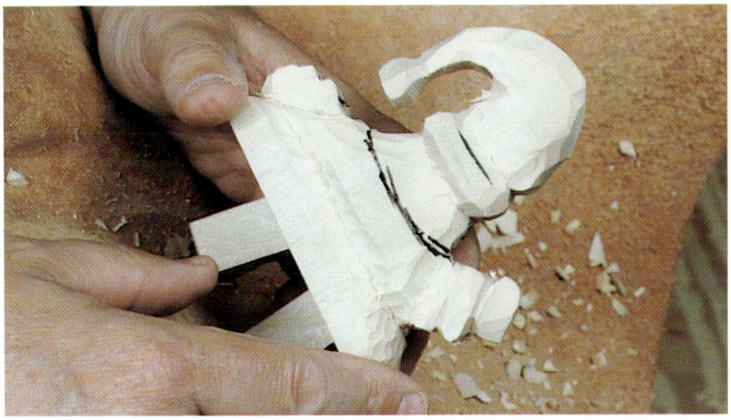

Draw in the line that defines the bottom of the hair.

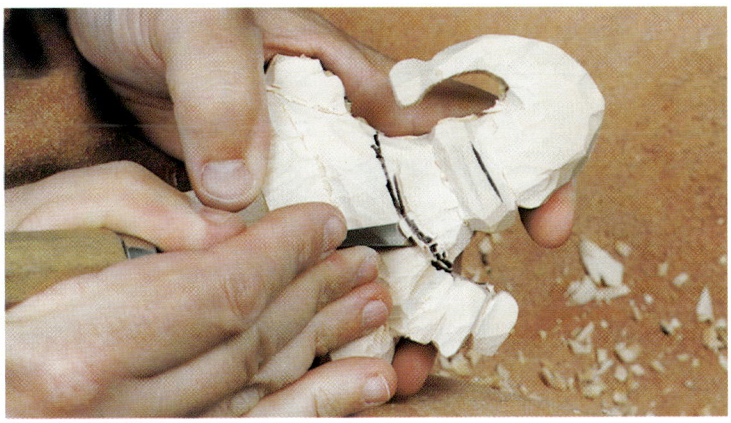

Make a stop cut along the bottom of the hair and then remove the hair up to the stop cut.

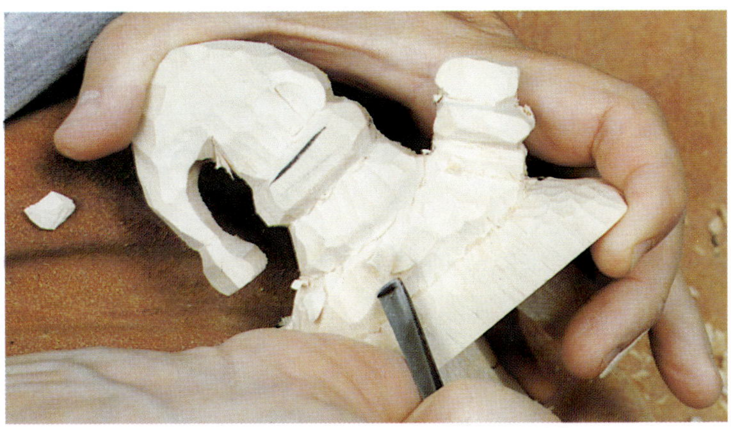

Remove some of the coat to make it smaller. This also helps to define the hairline more.

Cut the fur cuff lines on the front.

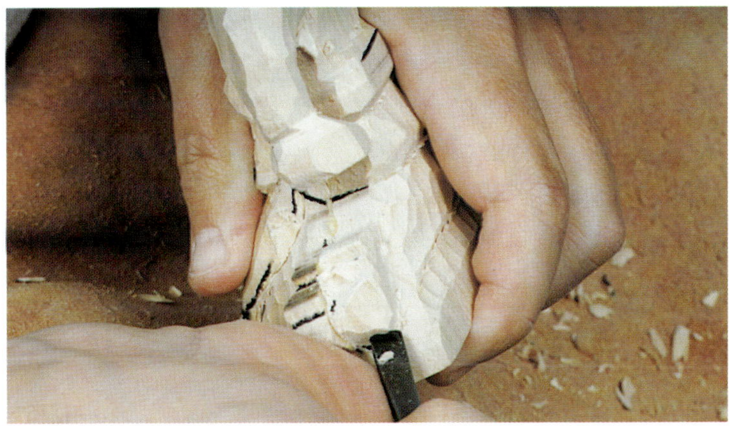

Remove wood to shape the arm and hand.

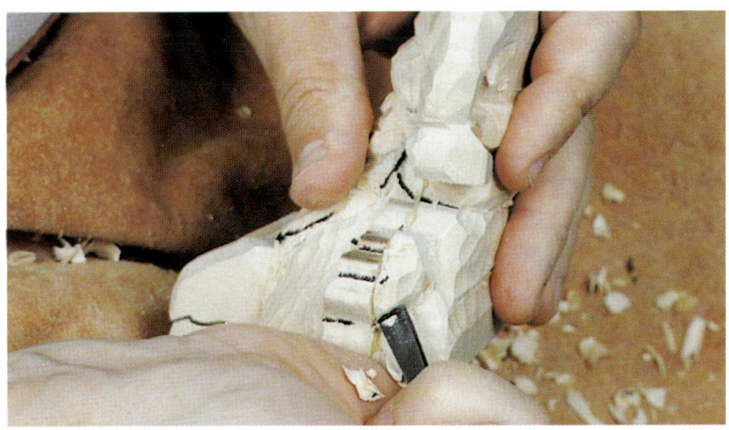

Remove more wood from the arm.

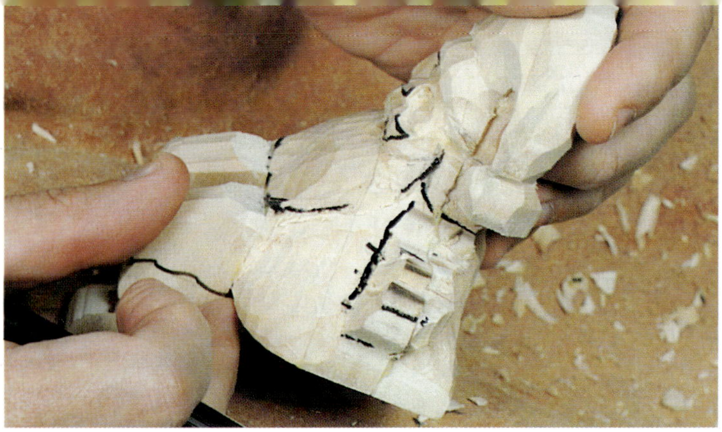

Redraw the lines defining the arm and body separation.

Make the cut defining the top of the boot fur. Note: Please be careful when cutting on the legs. Even if you have doweled the legs onto the body they could pop off when you put maximum pressure on the knife - and that would be a problem.

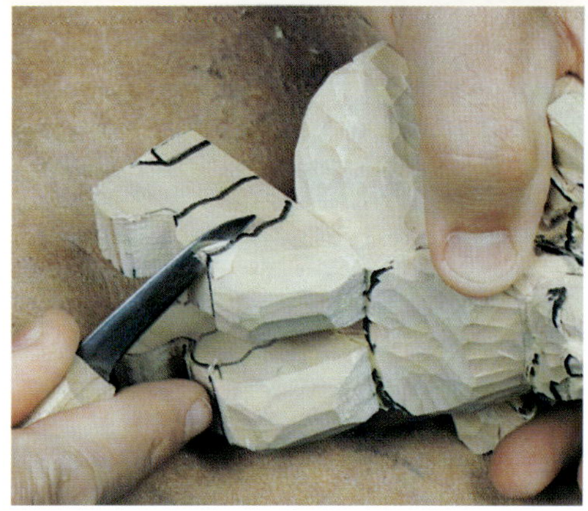

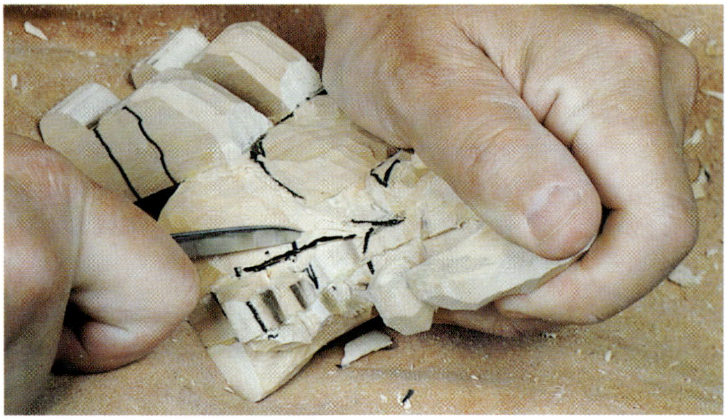

Cut the line to define the separation.

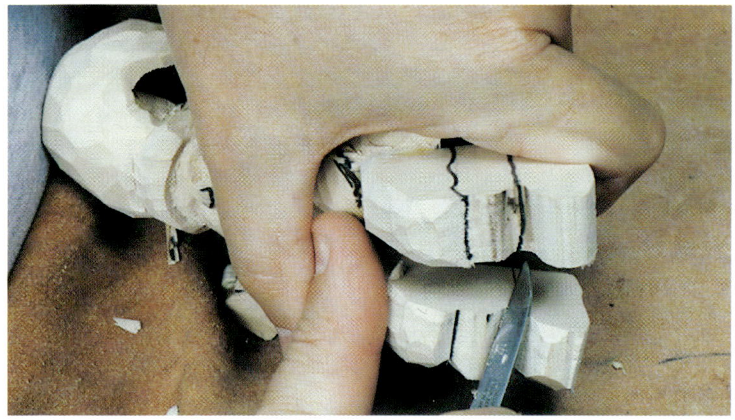

Shape the fur at the top of the boot.

Draw the line separating the back of the arm from the coat.

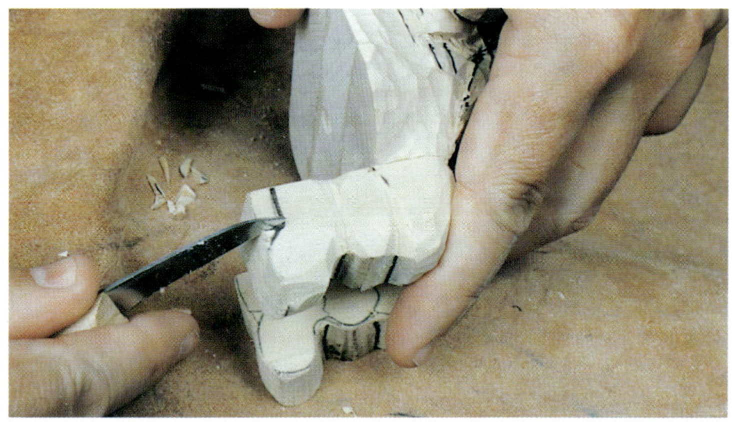

Cut the triangle that defines the heel separation from the sole of the boot.

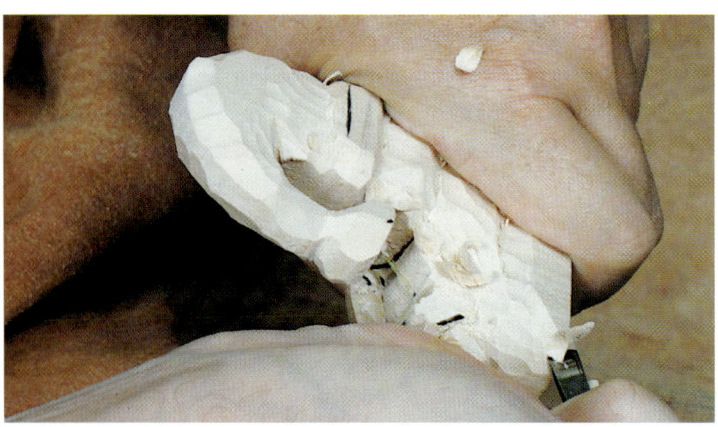

Shape the fur at the bottom of the back. Also, cut wood away below the arm.

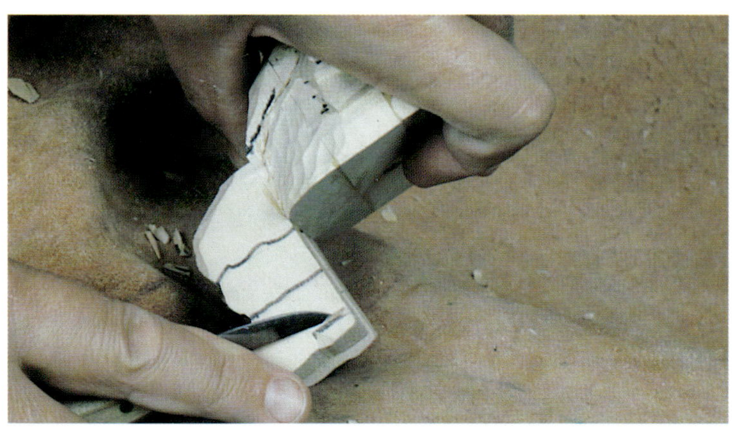

Cut the top of the heel.

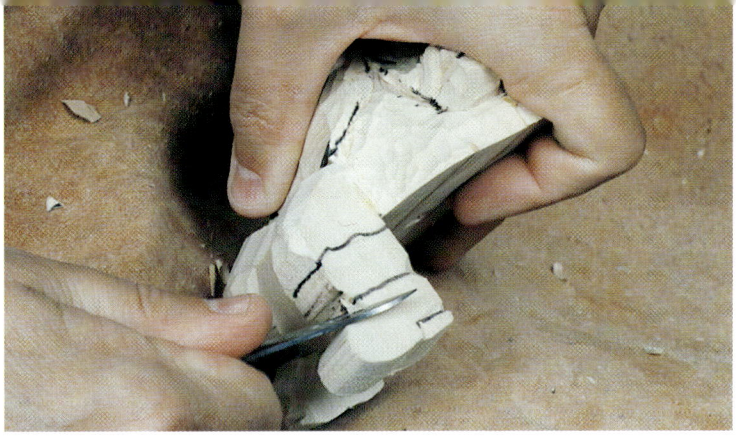
Cut the line at the top of the foot.

Cut the other boot the same way.

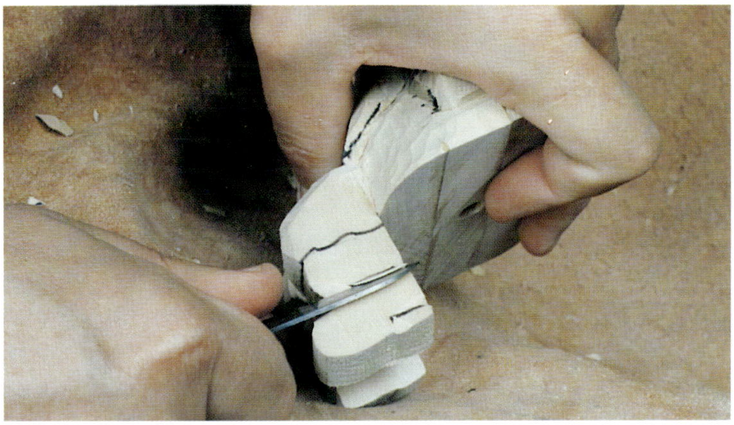
Cut the line all the way to the back.

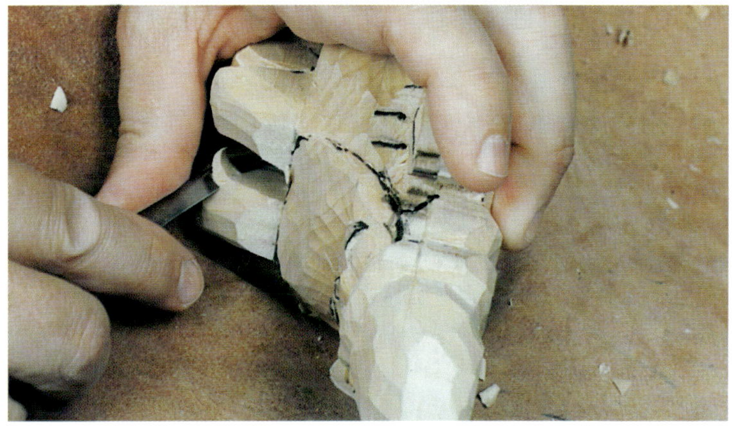
Shape the inside edges of the legs.

The is the way the piece looks now.

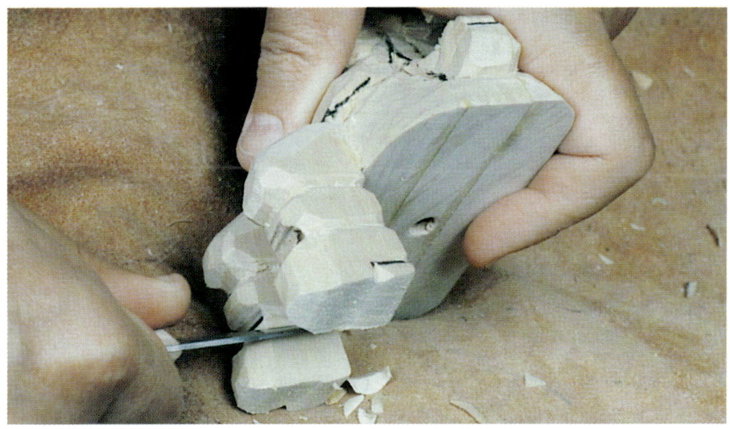
Shape the inside edges of the boots.

Cut the insides of the boots.

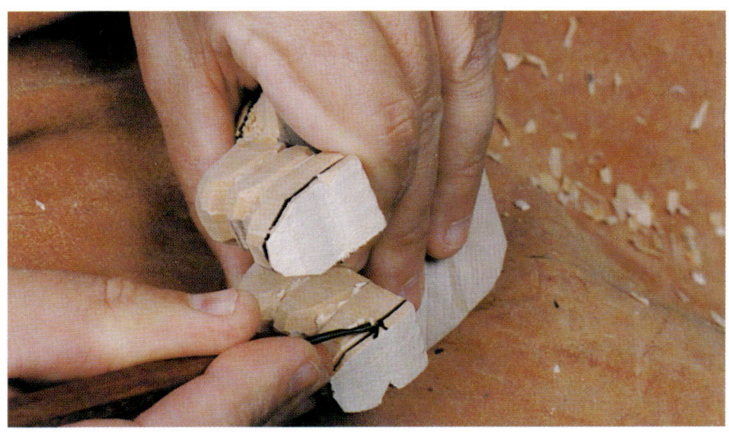
Here, I am using a small "V" gouge to cut the lines that go inside between the legs. You can also use a knife.

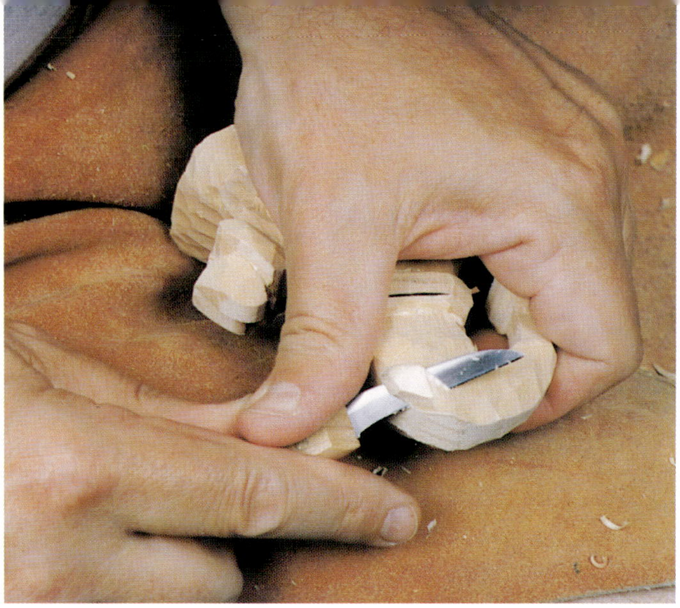

Go back over the piece shaping any unshaped areas, like those on the hat.

The lines seen here define the top and bottom of the belt and the top of the fur trim.

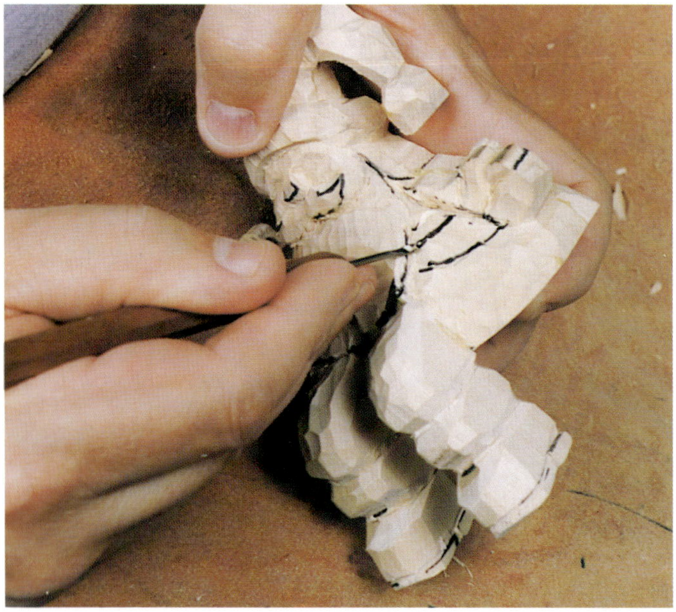

Cut along the top and bottom of the belt.

Cut the line along the top of the fur trim.

Here, I cut the lines that simulate the fur of the trim. I use a small "V" gouge, but you can use a knife.

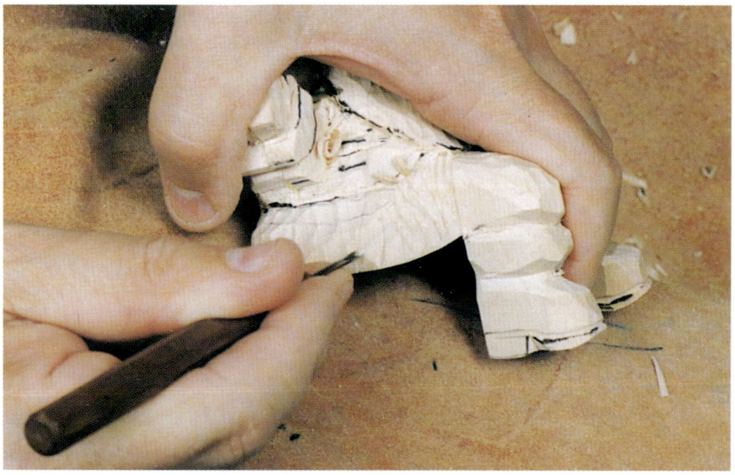

Cut the trim all the way around.

The fur trim goes all the way around.

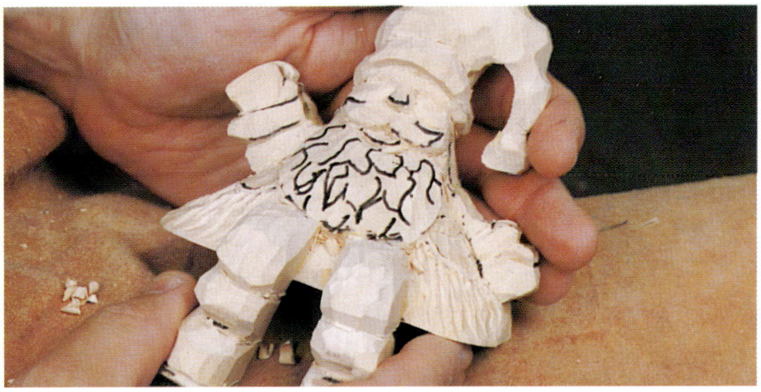

Draw on the beard. In the design notes, I gave other examples of the different beard types. Select the type of beard you want and draw it on.

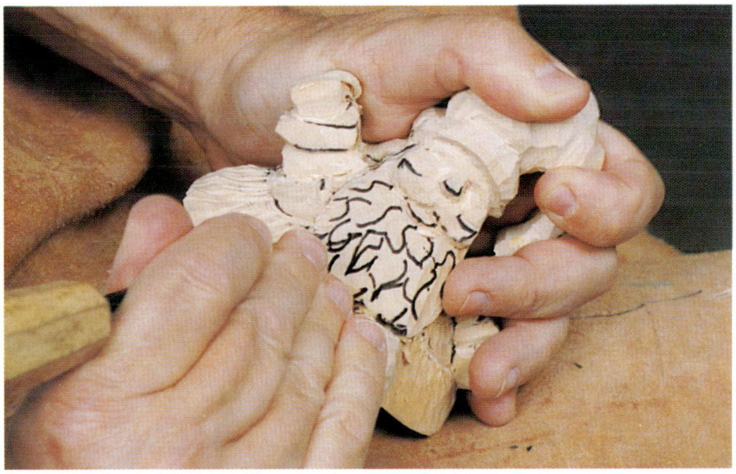

I use a shallow "U" gouge to cut the lines down into the beard. A knife also works well.

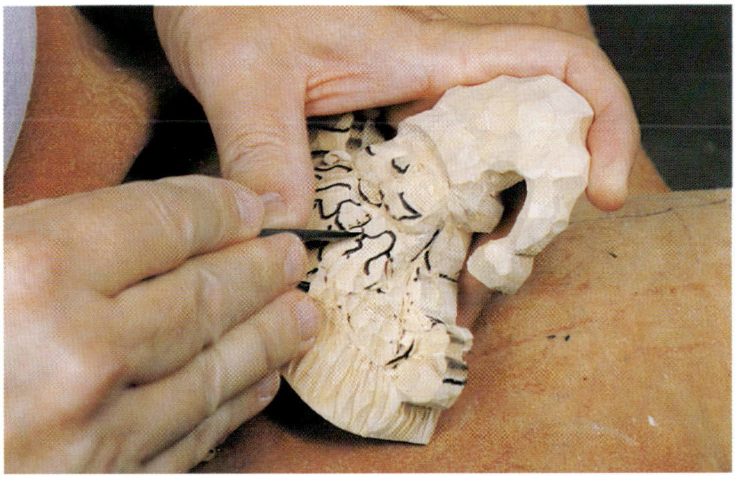

More beard work.

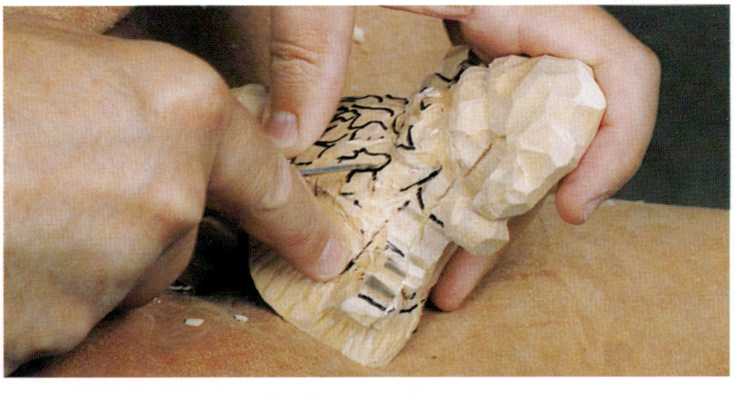

Here, I am using a knife to work on the beard.

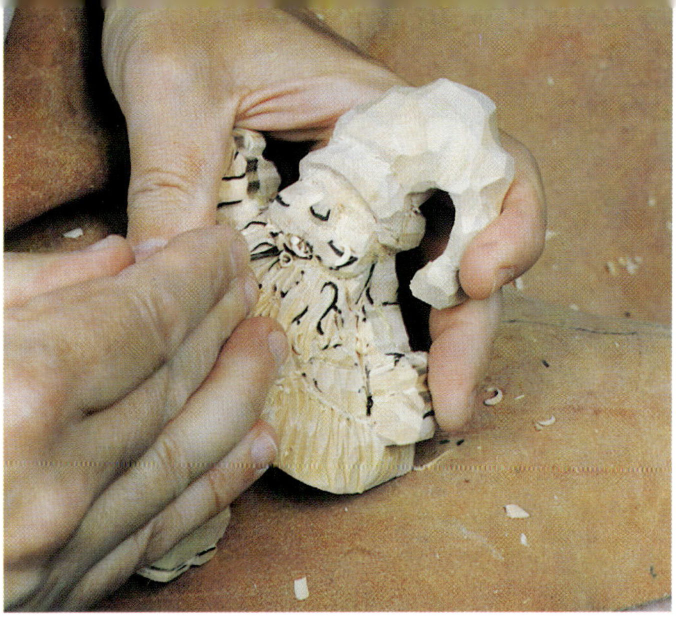

I cut a deep "V" cut along each of the black lines on the beard. It may take a couple of tries to get it to look right.

I use a small "V" gouge to create the hair on the beard, but a knife can be used too. The hair lines are not cut as deep as the separating cuts in the beard. This gives a multi-layer look to the beard.

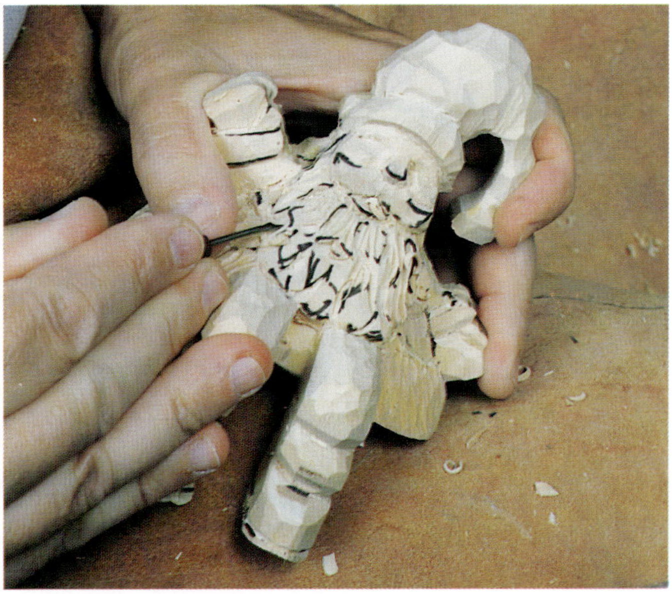

View of beard with more cuts to simulate hair.

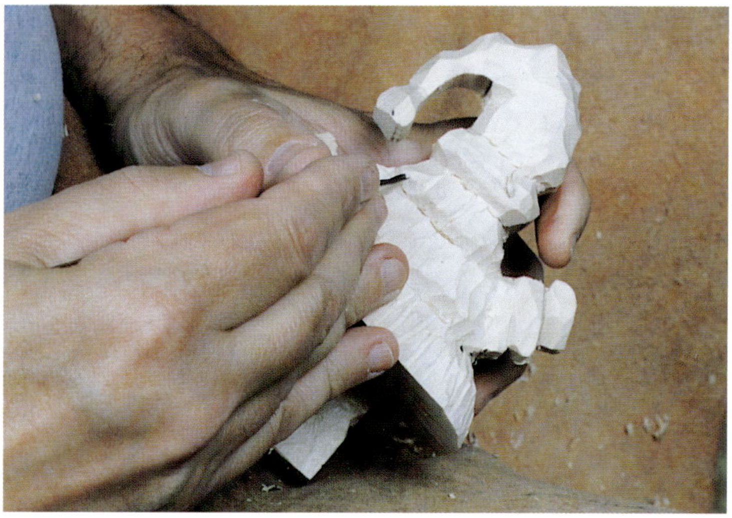

I use the small "V" gouge to put the hair lines on. Because the hair is put on instead of taken off, this is known as a "reverse hair cut." You could maybe call this the "Rogaine" move.

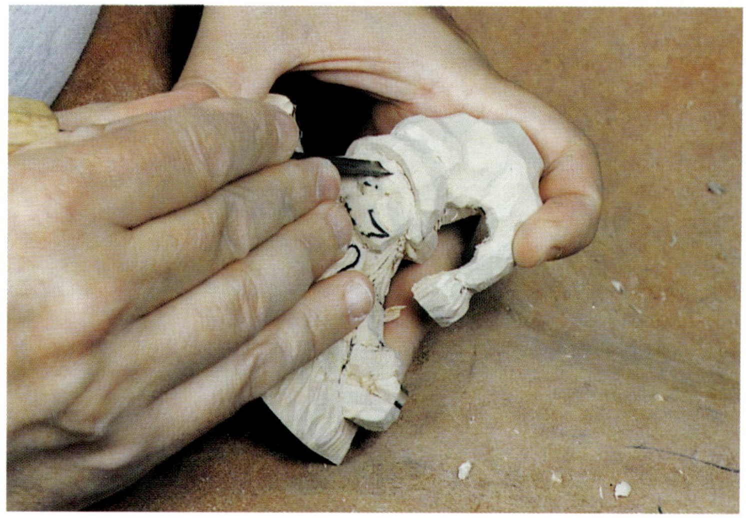

I also deepened the line at the bottom of the hat to highlight the face.

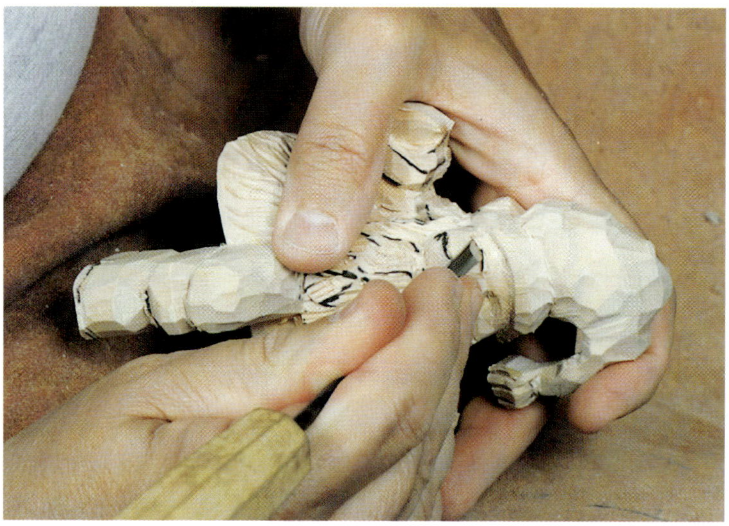

This is the way the piece looks at the end of the carving. From here, use a Foredom rotating tool to clean it up and do the final shaping.

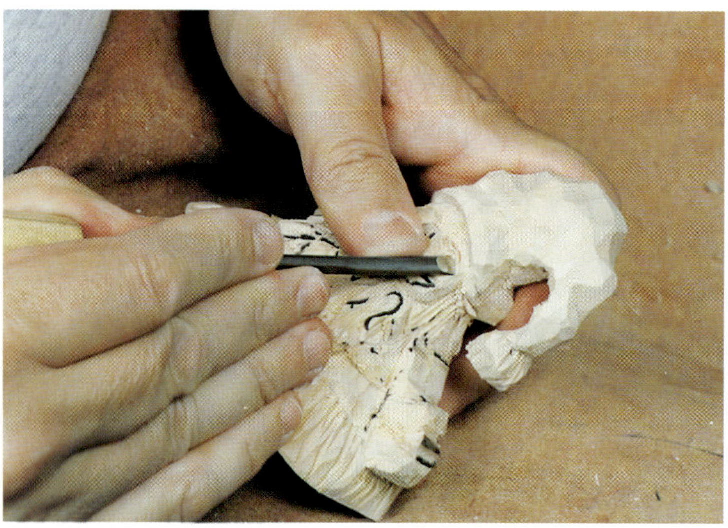

I decided to deepen the eye sockets. You can use your own judgment and deepen the eye sockets as you wish.

A view of the back of the piece before smoothing/sanding.

After it has been sanded and base coated, the piece should look like this. I sand the piece by hand with at least 2 different grits - the last one is 400 wet/dry - and use "White Lightning" for the base coating. Sometimes there is additional light sanding required after the base coating.

Back view. Note: On this piece I wanted it to be more "in the round," so I went ahead and cut the belt into the back to make the back look finished. Most of the pieces in the collection, however, have plain backs in order to keep costs down.

This view shows the piece on his back so you can see the top of the hat.

Side view of base coated piece.

This is the bottom of the piece. You can see clearly the glue lines from the build up of the various layers. The hole is from the carver's screw.

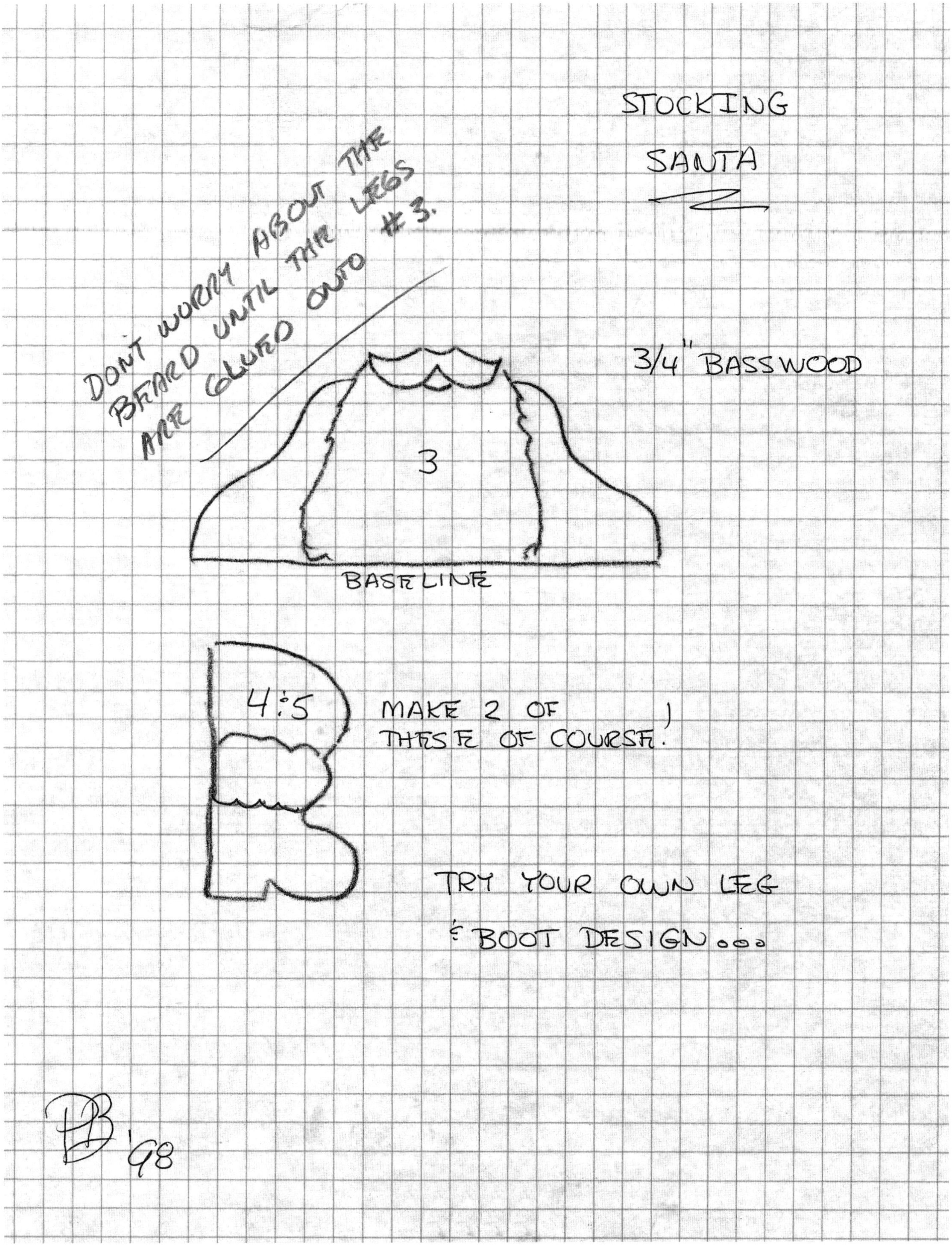
STOCKING
SANTA
DONT WORRY ABOUT THE
BEARD UNTIL THE LEGS
ARE GLUED ONTO #3.
3/4" BASSWOOD
3
BASELINE
4:5
MAKE 2 OF
THESE OF COURSE!
TRY YOUR OWN LEG
& BOOT DESIGN...
PB '98

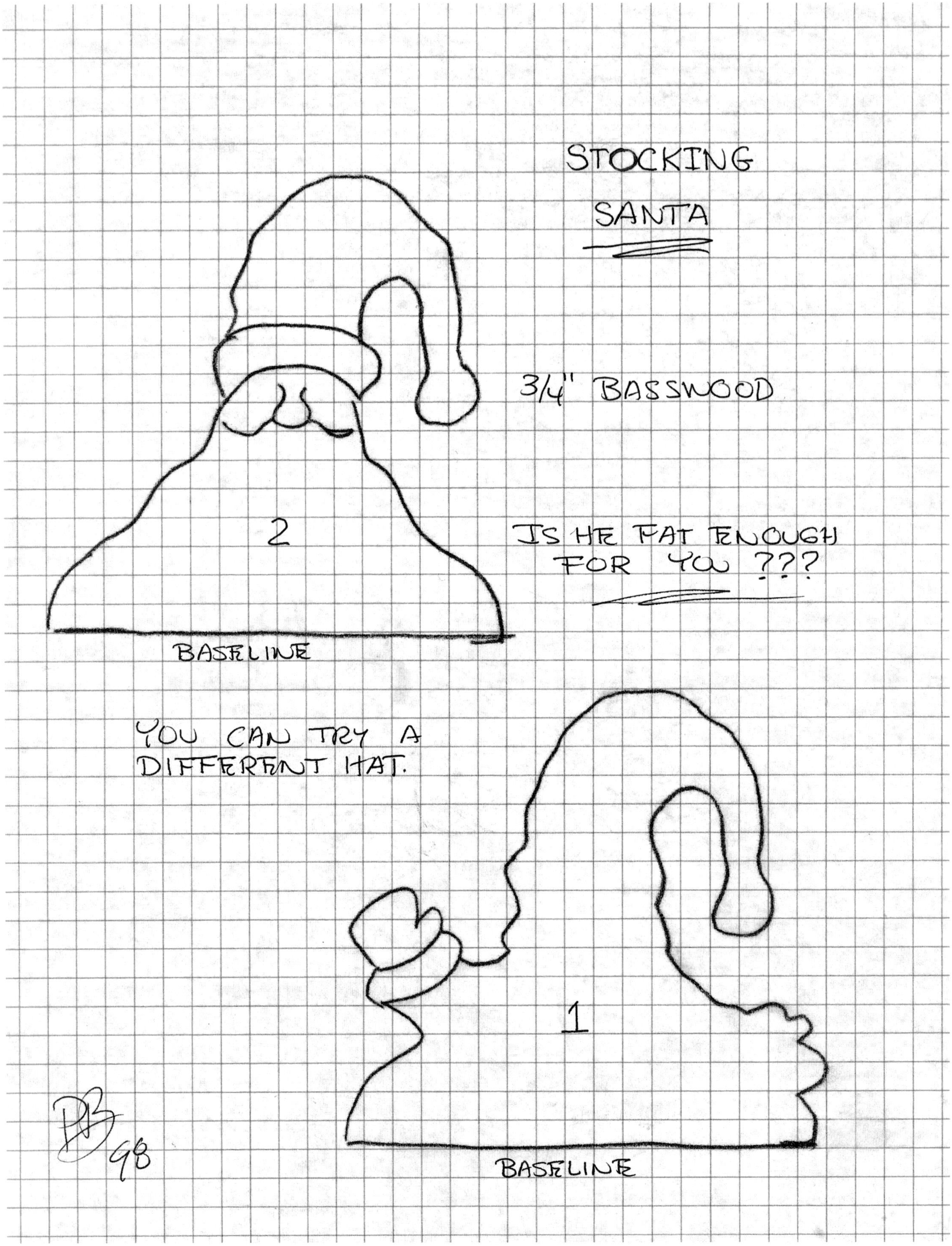
STOCKING SANTA
3/4" BASSWOOD
2
IS HE FAT ENOUGH FOR YOU ???
BASELINE
YOU CAN TRY A DIFFERENT HAT.
1
BASELINE

Chapter 4
Painting the Santa

The first thing the eye sees in these pieces is color. Because they are intended to be displayed on shelves where there are lots of things competing for attention, we wanted very bright intense colors to be used for these pieces. The little details and extra items Camille added help draw attention to the pieces and definitely give each one a unique look.

The craft acrylic paints Camille used for these projects provided the intense color we wanted while also allowing us to take advantage of their quick drying time. Very little mixing of colors was done in order to maintain consistency, and often Camille used paint "right out of the bottle" when she could.

To seal the wood, an undercoat was added to the pieces, which would allow the pieces to be painted in one coat. Occasionally, there is a need for an additional coat to get the depth of color desired.

You don't need to use her exact colors for the projects. Try your own color combinations. I encourage you too to add your own "extras" to the pieces. I think of it as "the more the merrier." However, we have to keep our additions under control because the added items increase the cost in commercial manufacturing. If it weren't for those constraints, we would be more extravagant too!

The Santa is now ready for painting. The entire piece was sealed with a product called "White Lightning," a stain and sealer made by J. W. Etc. that gives a whitewashed look to the item. We use it to help define the white areas of the piece. After the sealer has dried, spray the piece with a light coat of Grumbacher Final Fixative (Matte Finish), creating a smoother sealed surface to paint on. Camille used Ceramcoat Delta paints for the project. "Fleshtone" is used for the face and lips and allowed to dry.

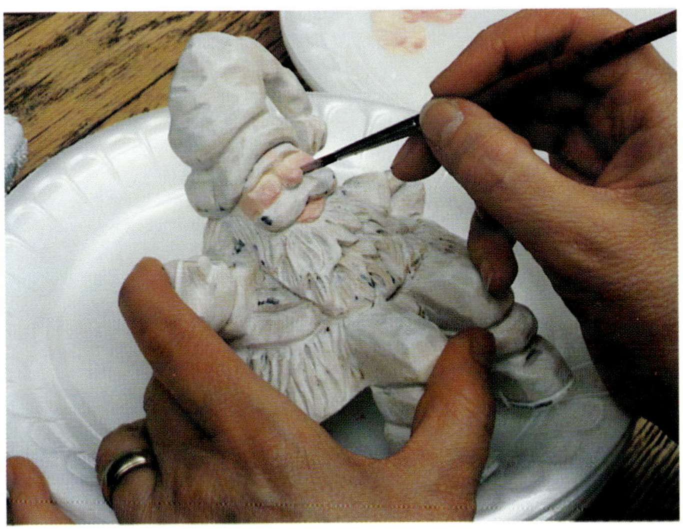

Blend "Fleshtone" with a drop of "Berry Red" and use this shade to highlight the cheeks and lips. This gives Santa that rosy look he likes.

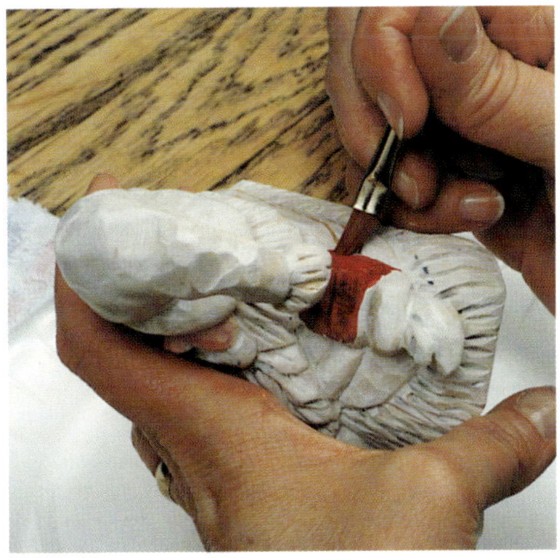

"Bright Red" is used to color in the large areas of the coat, hat, and legs of the pants. Camille applies the red quickly with the idea that the areas between colors will be cleaned up later.

This view shows the red of the coat, hat, and pants.

The back view shows the red on the coat and hat.

View of the back of the boots. Note: The black will be used to color the belt in front and back also. After the black has dried, a light spray of final fixative is applied to make it easier to "fine tune" the separated areas of color.

While Santa's polka dots are drying, cut a Christmas stocking from 1/4" basswood, sand it, and base coat it with the "White Lightning."

Black is used for the boots.

"White" paint has been used to cover the areas for the beard and the fur of the cuffs, coat, and boots. To "clean up" the lines where the red and white meet, Camille used the white paint. Yes, this is the same color red as before but somehow it came out differently in the photo processing.

"Christmas Green" is used to cover the main area of the stocking.

Front view of the boots after black is applied.

Here, Camille uses the opposite end of her brush dipped in "White" to add polka dots to Santa's mittens and hat. Thin the paint slightly with a little water or acrylic extender. Finish applying the polka dots and set the piece aside to dry.

The green is cut in carefully.

Top left: The stocking has been put aside to dry. A light application of "Bridgeport Gray", thinned with a little water, is used as a light topcoat on the beard. This highlights the deeper cuts much like "antiquing" would.

Top center: "Peyne's Grey" put on the fur trim of the hat in elongated strokes or ovals will create the appearance of dark highlights on the fur. Thin the grey a bit with water for a softer look.

Top right: "White" polka dots on the green areas of the stocking add highlights and coordinate well with the pattern on Santa's hat and mittens.

The gray goes on the mustache too.

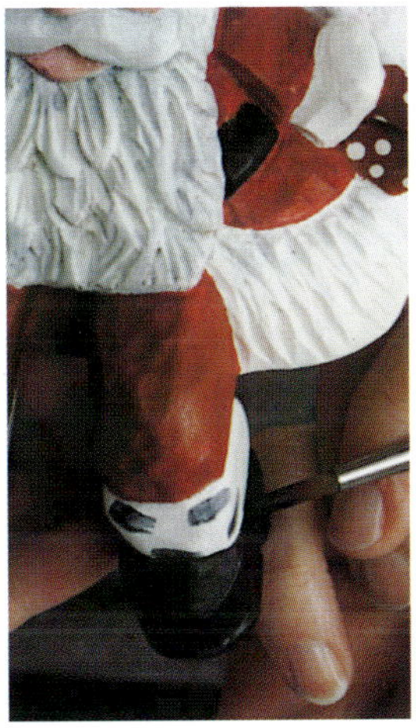

The same treatment is used for the fur at the top of the boots.

Above: Here is Santa at this point. Note that red was added between his legs because, were he wearing a real coat, the white fur would go up and over the legs revealing his red pants underneath.

Below right: Camille drills a tiny hole in Santa's mittened hand to hold the wire for his stocking.

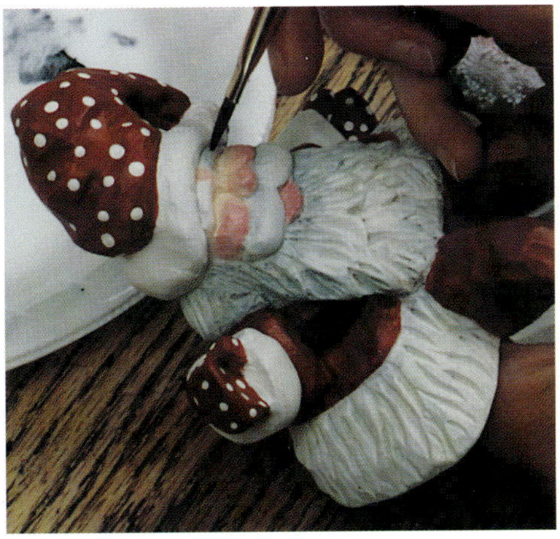

And on the eyebrows.

Return to the Christmas stocking and apply "White" to the top and toe areas.

Common wire was used to help Santa hold up his stocking.

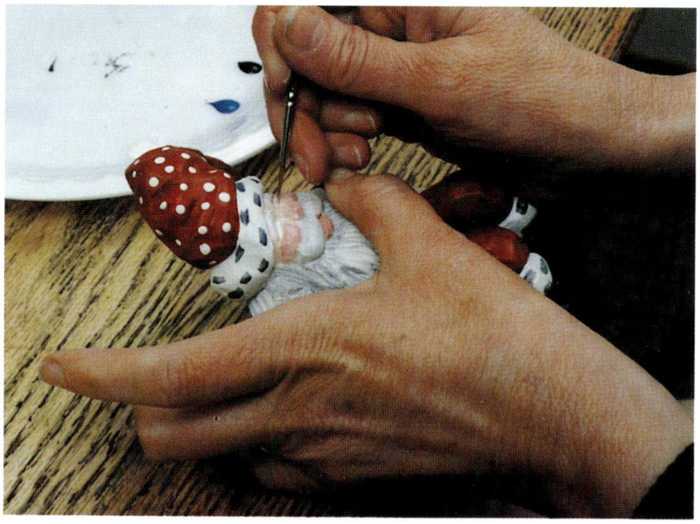

It is time for Santa to get some eyes. A slash of "White" is applied as the base coat for each eye.

This close-up shows the basic eye structure. Since I left the sockets smooth, there were no carved details for Camille to follow. The advantage to this is Camille can fit the eyes in as she sees them rather than having to "paint between the lines" of a carved eye. First, apply a white underlayer and let it dry. A blue oval is then painted over the dry white area. Camille used "Copen Blue" lightened with "White."

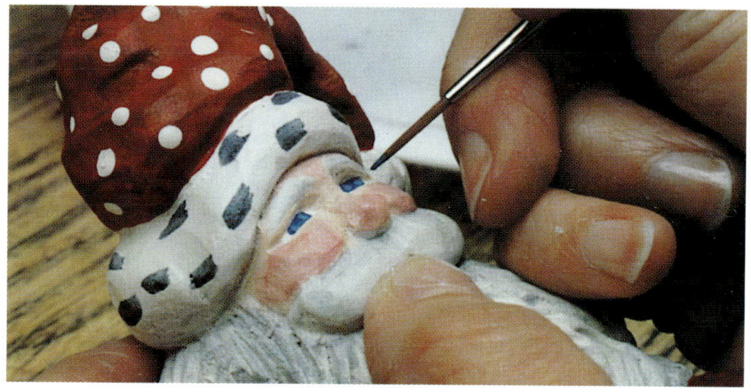

A black dot is placed in the center of the blue oval, and "Copen Blue," straight from the bottle, is added around the light blue.

Here, you can see the layers - white underlayer, light blue oval, darker blue lines, black dot.

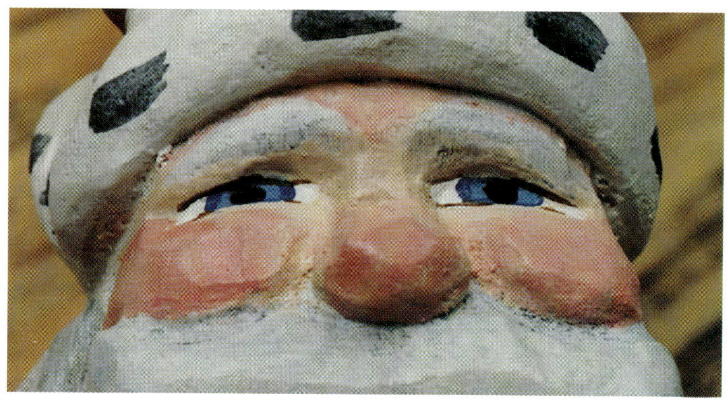

A thin line of "Burnt Umber" can be added at the top and bottom of each eye as an enhancement, making Santa appear more bright-eyed.

A white highlight in each eye creates the illusion of wetness or reflected light and is the finishing touch added to the eyes. At this point you should apply a coat of Grumbacher Final Fixative to seal the piece and provide a matte finish. Please read the instructions for the spray. It must be used in a well ventilated area that is within the temperature range specified on the can.

Chapter 5
The Gallery

Front and back view of the painted Santa.

Side views of the painted Santa.

Close-up view of the front.

Another grouping. Study these for a moment and think about how you can change the designs to make them more personal.

A small grouping of the jolly fellows. I hope this will inspire you to make more than one of these shelf sitting Christmas celebrants.

One last grouping.

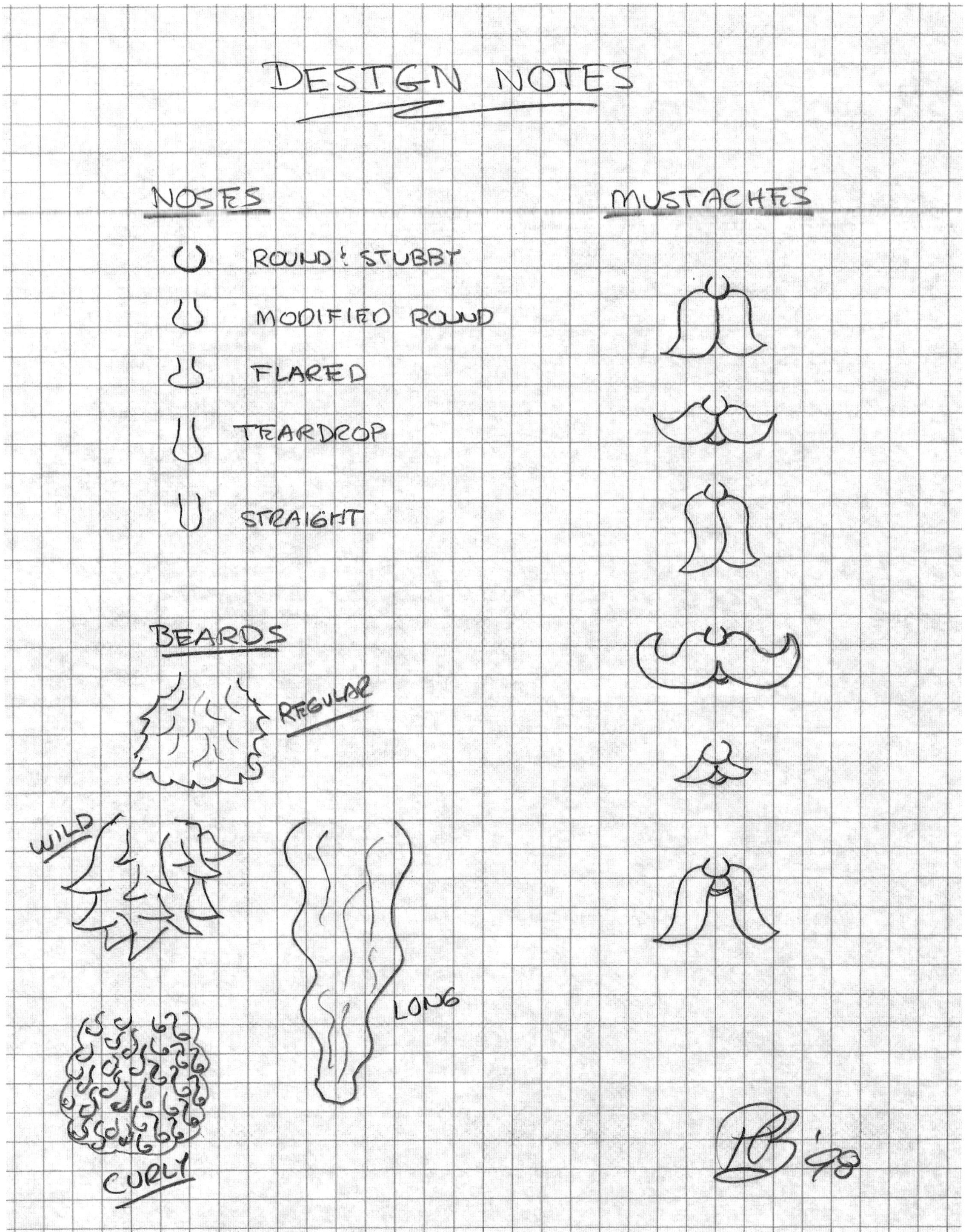
DESIGN NOTES
NOSES
ROUND & STUBBY
MODIFIED ROUND
FLARED
TEARDROP
STRAIGHT
MUSTACHES
BEARDS
REGULAR
WILD
LONG
CURLY
'98

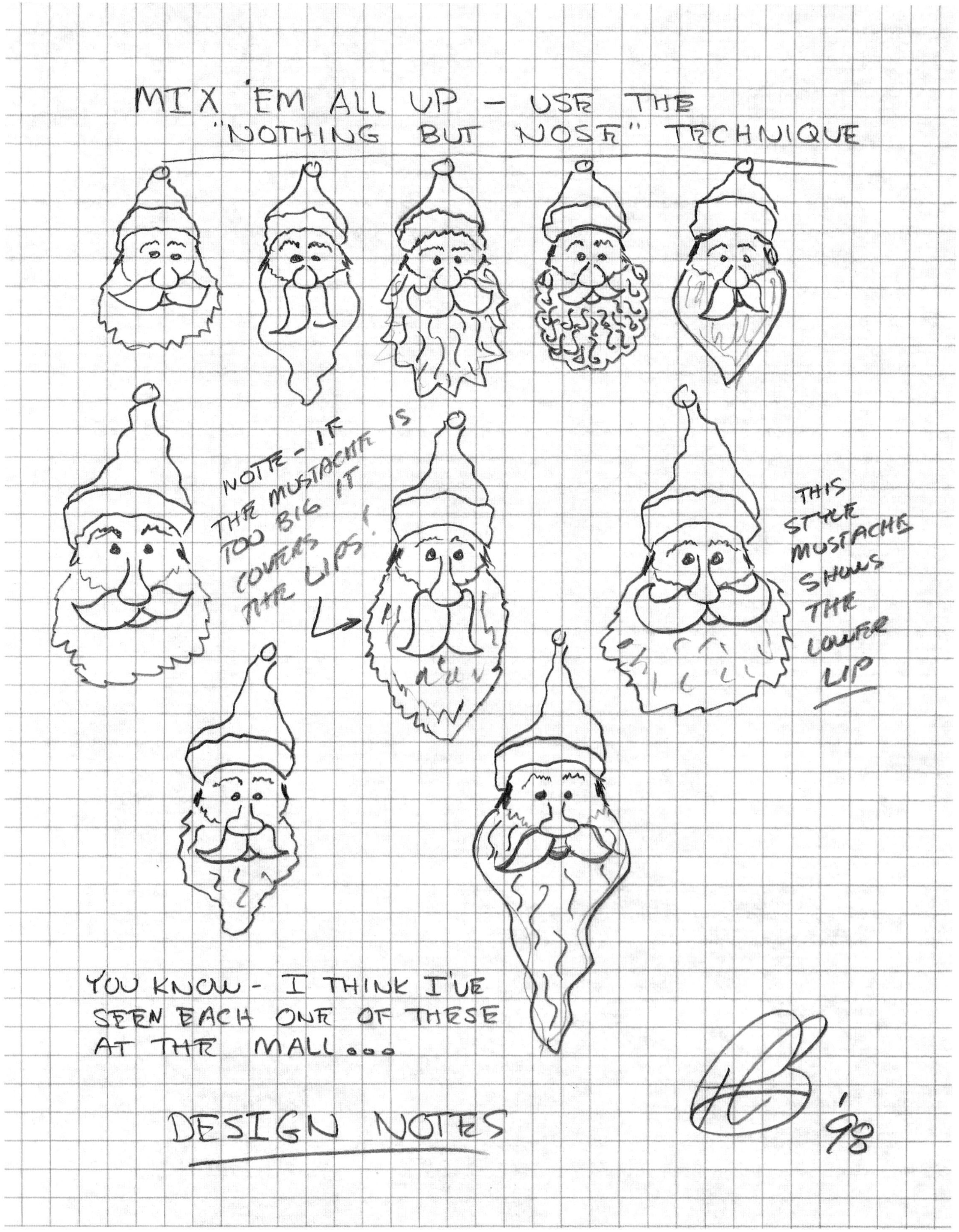
MIX 'EM ALL UP - USE THE "NOTHING BUT NOSE" TECHNIQUE
NOTE - IF THE MUSTACHE IS TOO BIG IT COVERS THE LIPS!
THIS STYLE MUSTACHE SHOWS THE LOWER LIP
YOU KNOW - I THINK I'VE SEEN EACH ONE OF THESE AT THE MALL...
DESIGN NOTES
'98

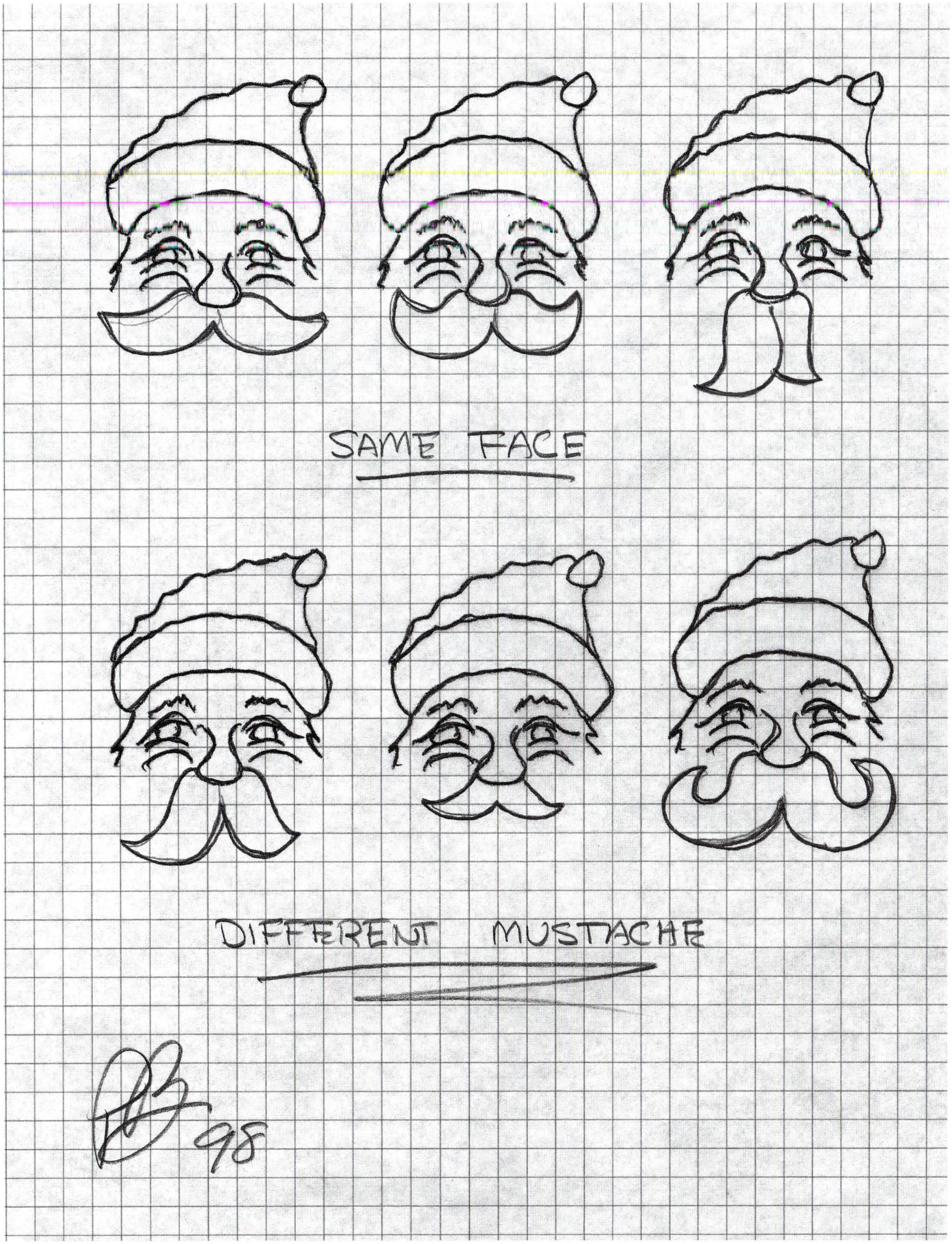
SAME FACE
DIFFERENT MUSTACHE
98

SIX FACES - SIX DIFFERENT BEARDS -

SANTA SPENDS THE DAY AT "THE BEARD WEARHOUSE" TRYING ON DIFFERENT STYLES.